REACHING FOR THE GOLD

By Everett Beich

Beich Publications
Chico, CA

TABLE OF CONTENTS

MOUNTAIN GOOD

"I can't!" said I,
as on the slopes of
Mountain Good
I stood.

"You can!" spoke the
mountain back to me.
"You can, if you
only would."

"I WANT to climb
you, Mountain Good, but
don't know where
to start."

"You start at the
bottom, like the rest,
and climb with all
your heart."

I start to
climb you, Mountain Good.
It is a long
hard climb.

I climb and hear
you say, "That's good!
Just keep your goal
in mind."

"I can just go
part way," said I.
"Right here I'll have
to stop."

"You made it here.
Now keep on climbing
'till you reach
the top."

So on I climb
Up to the top of
Mountain Good,
you see.

And now I look
around me and am
pleased, so pleased
with ME!

Written by:
Carol O. Keller

i

ABOUT THE AUTHOR

Everett Beich was born to German immigrants in the Midwest during the Depression. His father was a barber in the small community of Kulm, North Dakota. As a boy, he knew nothing about running water, indoor plumbing, or paved streets. He learned to work about the same time he learned to walk. His mother and father taught him, early in his life, the importance of work, and that work meant survival. Everett always had jobs after school hours, and at the age of thirteen, his summer vacations were spent working away from home on local farms.

Although he did not do well in school, he became quite successful in later years, through hard work and careful planning. Today Beich is a multimillionaire who credits his success to finding, and using, his "gifted abilities."

After serving his country in World War II, The author decided to go to college and become a pharmacist. He soon learned that was an occupation which would not suit him, but upon enrolling at a small business college, he finally found something in school that he enjoyed. To his surprise, he made very good grades and, after completing his business courses, he tried his hand at real estate sales. Because of his longstanding ability to work hard, he was soon one of the top listing agents and salespersons in the office. He says that this was for no other reason than all the other salespeople were used to working regular hours, while he knew nothing about an eight-to-four job.

Meanwhile, Beich tried building homes and farming, both of which, through no fault of his own, took every cent he had made in real estate. He did not, however, let these setbacks discourage him; in fact, through them he learned much about business that he was able to use to his advantage. He then went into the grocery business and succeeded, building his small store into a supermarket.

After seven years, he sold his store and moved to California, where he went into mobile home sales. Through the years, he invested in mobile home parks, commercial properties, shopping centers, almond orchards, and oil ventures. He is one of the original founders, Vice Chairman of the Board of Directors, and one of the major stockholders of the Tri Counties Bank, which now has a chain of fourteen branches throughout northern California.

Writing this book has been a new venture for the author, as has his recent establishing of a manufacturing company, the fulfillment of a long-time dream. He says he wears many hats, venturing into unfamiliar areas and succeeding by following his natural abilities, working hard, and taking time to plan. Each area is, in its own way, just as exciting as the other. And while he is wearing these hats, you can be sure he is dreaming, planning, and working on other ventures.

Beich maintains that, with a lot of planning ahead and hard work, a person can be prepared for whatever comes along. Becoming wealthy, he adds, is not that difficult and can be fun. If people can learn to enjoy some of their hardships as well as their successes, it will take away much of the burden and create enthusiasm. The author says he can never promise it will be easy, but he stresses repeatedly that, while people will earn every dollar they make, they can make a game out of it.

Beich shows his readers that in real estate, in farming, in investments, in mobile home parks and sales, in banking, and in manufacturing, he continually faced new challenges, wore new hats, and wore them well. His goal in life is to fit his readers with new hats and equip them to wear those hats well. He wants his readers to succeed, to reach for the Gold!

DEDICATION

I would like to dedicate this book to the memory of my father, who died in 1967.

When I was a young man in high school, I asked him if I could go to college to become an optometrist.

His response? "You work, not go to school."

His decision, at that time, changed the course of my life. Because of that decision, I learned to work, and learning to work became the key to my success.

I would also like to dedicate this book to all parents who take time to influence and teach their children the importance of work. Making a child work is not punishment or lack of love. In contrast, the parents are showing how much they love their children and want them to succeed. I hope each parent who reads this book will acquire guidelines to teach their children to work and realize the importance of it. A parent's influence never ends. It lasts throughout a child's lifetime and for generations to come.

ACKNOWLEDGEMENTS

I would like to express my appreciation to Carol Keller for the inspiration and help she has given me. People having similar circumstances in business, or, as in this instance, in writing a book, are often willing to help you and never want to take money for it, or even a "thank you." Her help was very valuable, and I could never have succeeded without it.

With that in mind, I want to thank all the people who helped me when I needed help just getting this book started, as well as those who edited, published, and printed it.

A special thanks to my Mother and Father for their effort in teaching me the importance of work and life.

A special remembrance to "Old Man Murray," who left me with two principles of life which I shall never forget: (1) Enjoy your children, for they are your special part of life; and, (2) Live your life to the utmost each day for some day you will wake up, look in the mirror, and find yourself to be an old man. Life is precious, don't waste it.

INTRODUCTION

EVERY PERSON HAS THE RIGHT TO SUCCEED!

REACHING FOR THE GOLD is proof that success is possible. This book will encourage as well as direct anyone who wants to find success.

It is a book of examples, so the reader can easily understand it. It gives tangible ideas and instances, rather than theories for success which apply to everyone in general and no one in particular.

This book is simple and easy to read. I have tried to keep in mind all types of readers, from all backgrounds and educational levels. Through this book I will show you that you can be successful whether or not you made good grades in school. Good grades alone do not ensure success. Most people do not get graded on their gifted ability which they should be using to succeed in life.

I have often been contacted by people who ask me how I became successful and who want advice on how to achieve their own success. The main purpose of writing this book is to give sound, practical advice, along with some of my own personal experience with success: how to obtain it, keep it, and deal with it.

Anyone can adapt this book to their life and understand it. I want you to understand the inner workings of success.

Thousands of people are reaching for success, looking for knowledge and knowhow, wanting someone to help them get started, needing that extra push to stimulate them into being successful. My book is unique, it's different. As you read it, you too will become excited and anxious to put into your everyday life the principles of success and begin REACHING FOR THE GOLD.

Do you have questions like this: What type of venture is good for me? Do I have to go into something totally new to succeed? Is there something I can do better than anyone else? Can I use that ability to achieve success? How? Where does the courage come from that makes a person successful?

If you are the type of person who doesn't think about how many hours you have to work or what you have to accomplish to make the money you want, this book is for you. You will be extremely hard to hold back because you will be continually working, planning, and educating yourself.

Some of you may have experienced the ghetto. Some may feel like you are in the ghetto or may not be succeeding as you had hoped you would be. Others may be successful but still unhappy and wanting more. You are the one I want to reach and inspire. Are you tired of not having the money, the car, the home, the travel, the clothes or personal belongings you want? Are you tired of having your dreams always out of reach? I want to help you find your gifted ability, get you to work and reach for the Gold. When you find your dream and believe in yourself, you will find success.

Remember, as you reach out, your venture has to out-weigh everything else in your life. Although your present goal may be to own a Ferrari, or to play golf or tennis every day, that goal should not supercede your ultimate goal. Your ultimate goal must be to make your life successful. It will take you many hours of hard work and planning to reach your final goal.

In this book, I share my personal experiences. You will see I had my ups and downs, some hard times, some good times, lots of hard work and some luck. Without the hard work and determination, I would not have had the luck.

Here is my simple Formula for Success. As you read this book, I want you to think about it and begin to use it.

HARD WORK	=	BUSINESS
BUSINESS	=	PROFITS
PROFITS	=	INVESTMENTS
INVESTMENTS	=	EXCESS INCOME
EXCESS INCOME	=	RICHES AND SUCCESS

To you, who hold your future in your hand, I present my book. It is a simple manual which will direct your thinking and chart your course to success. May you, as you read, find courage to use the practical information given here. Good luck. There is a prosperous future lying ahead for you, REACHING FOR THE GOLD!

PART I

SUCCESS AND YOU

1

KNOWING YOURSELF

This book is about you! It is about how you can prepare yourself to make money and what to do once you start making it. It is not on what investments to make. When you have finished reading, I want you to become a self-made man or woman, a self-made successful person, possibly even a self-made millionaire.

Have you ever stood in a snowbank, taken two steps backwards, looked at those footprints, and wondered if you really knew that person who made them?

Knowing yourself is the first qualification for being successful. In this chapter, we will be looking at the type of person you are. Everyone has the qualifications for success. The question is, are you willing to sacrifice and work hard enough at what you are qualified to do in order to obtain that success? You must discipline yourself before you can achieve success.

In your discovery of yourself, it is okay to find and take short-cuts, but don't do it at the expense of your success. People have a tendency to be lazy. They try to get by with something less than the best. Whatever I do, I try to do the very best I know how. If I cannot put my best into it, I would rather not do it at all, because I am frustrating my own sense of accomplishment. When you determine to tackle a project, always do it to the best of your ability.

Are you presently employed? Do you like your job? Or do you wake up in the morning and say to yourself, "Oh, no. Another day of work. I hate this job!" Yet, because you have responsibilities, you get out of bed and go to work. Some days aren't so bad, while others are absolutely terrible, and you find yourself thinking, "Surely I am worth more than this."

Sometimes you sit back and think, "If I were the head of this

1

department, I would change the system and, therefore, get more productivity." But the rub comes again. You are not the head. Only an employee, and an underpaid one at that!

And how about the times when you or one of your co-workers do a job really well, but when the boss comes around it is always the department head that gets the recognition. And you say to yourself, "If I were the department manager, I would make sure each person gets due recognition." Always dreaming, always making plans, but never seeming to be able to make those dreams and plans come true.

Maybe you are the department head, but you are underpaid, not getting ahead in life, and certainly not very happy. So, as another day ends, you go home tired and discouraged, having nothing better to offer.

Payday is great, always! You may go out for dinner, stop by a store to look around, and maybe even buy something. But the next day, you have to pay the bills. You are in the hole again. "Who should I pay this month? Can I afford to pay this one in full? Who is willing to wait a while for their money? What will happen if I don't pay this one? Why in the world can't I get ahead? Is this going to last forever?" The same old questions, and the same old answers. And your credit isn't getting any better.

But you have to work, and that is all there is to it. So you lock up your dreams again, and you go to work the next day, and the next, week after week, month after month, year after year, hoping against hope that someday, somewhere you will find the light at the end of that long, dark tunnel. Why wait? Success is not going to come to you! You have to make it happen.

If you fit into part or all of the above, you are most likely working at the wrong occupation. Each of us has a gifted ability. If you want to make a success of your life, as well as enjoy yourself while you are achieving your goals, you have to become aware of your gift and begin to use it. Finding your way out of the tunnel is possible. Once you discover yourself, it becomes much more attainable.

Or you may be one of the many who are unemployed, receiving a measly amount of money to try to live on from unemployment, disability, or welfare. You receive financial aid, but you are humiliated, degraded, and restless. It certainly is no fun, and you have little self-pride.

Let's give our life some meaning. Reach for some goals and not just dream about it. Make this the time of your life when you are going to reach out and get to that light, and stop saying that light is for someone else. Let's be sure that we do not listen to other people who tell us we can't have success. Nothing is impossible. In fact, once you get started you will find that it is not even difficult.

What are you waiting for? Are you waiting for a break? Waiting for the right time? Remember, it's never too late in life to start reaching for that light! But you must make it happen. There are people who do very little because they really feel they are not capable of doing more.

Take a moment to know yourself. What type of person are you? What do you really want in life? Are you happy with a Chevrolet, or do you want a Cadillac? Would you rather have a limousine and chauffeur? Do you want to fly commercial, or do you want to have your own private plane? Do you want a little sailboat, or do you want a yacht? Do you want a ranch or are you satisfied with renting and paying for someone else's success? You do have a choice. That choice is yours to make.

Are you really trying to be successful? Have you ever really tried? There are people who do nothing but wait for their government or unemployment checks each month. And yet they complain! No, not about themselves, but always about something or someone else. What a waste! Their chances for success are as good as anyone's, but they do not believe in themselves. They are afraid to try. They won't give themselves a chance.

Maybe that person is you. Be honest with yourself. Have you lost your self-confidence? Do you have habits which could destroy your potential for success? Are you unemployed because you drink too much, or are you using drugs? You must start pursuing a profitable life sometime, so why not rid yourself of your obstacles. Get off the drugs or alcohol. Take the responsibility for your position, rather than blaming your surroundings or society, and then work towards escaping from it. That tunnel may look long and forbidding to you, but if you look down it far enough, you can see the light! Start walking towards that golden pinpoint of light and eventually you will attain the Gold! You have to find your way out of the tunnel before you can start climbing your mountain. Most everyone starts at the bottom. If you wait to start big, you may never start at all.

You may be down and out, but don't let yourself stay down.

Find your ability by observing yourself and pursue your future from there.

Go look in the mirror. Be critical. Are you clean? Are your eyes clear? Is your body in good condition? Do you look like someone who wants to be successful? Would anyone who is successful want to be around you? We need to start somewhere. Let's start with this.

When you look better, you will feel better. When you look and feel like a business person, the next step is attitude. How is your frame of mind? Are you full of hate? Are you cocky? If so, you must change these areas of your life.

You may have to become less dependent on your parents. Even though most parents mean well, they have a tendency to be overprotective. This tendency to overprotect creates negative influences on their children. Being too close, or staying too close to your parents in later years, could limit your ability to achieve success.

FACT: It is alright to take advice from your parents, but you have to make your own success! Because humans are made to get away from their parents after a certain age, it is unhealthy to be overly dependent on them for support, whether emotional or financial. Sooner or later, you have to let go of that parental influence, try your own venture, and be yourself.

Now let's talk about changing you!

1. Do you let people manipulate you? Learn not to be manipulated. Be independent. Avoid complete dependence on anyone or anything.

2. How do you feel about yourself? Do you feel good? Can you hold your head up high and be proud?

3. Do you feel like working or do you feel run down? Do you feel lazy and just don't care? If so, find out why.

4. How late do you stay up? Get to bed early and get up early. One of the best things to get your body stimulated is a good morning walk or jog.

4

How far and fast depends on your age and condition. The longer you do it, the faster and farther you can jog. Give yourself time to think things out. You may need to be by yourself a short time each day.

5. You may want to stop smoking or drinking, or at least slow down. Get your body in shape, so you feel like doing good things.

6. Buy some nice clothes and keep them clean. Clothing does not have to be expensive to make you look good. Dress yourself to look sharp and prosperous. People like to associate and do business with successful people, so look successful.

7. Do not let anyone talk you into anything you don't want to do. So often people will do things to be liked or to make friends. Forget it! Those kinds of friends you do not need.

8. Don't listen to people who downgrade life and are depressing. Your surroundings also have a lot to do with your success. If your surroundings and the people around you are depressing--the good things in life are not appealing to them--you may need to move to a new environment and associate with people who will encourage rather than discourage you.

9. If you don't have a job, get one. Get any kind of job to start with, and go to work. Work hard. Work harder than anyone else and use this as your base to start your climb.

Once you find your job, pay very close attention to your thoughts and dreams while you're working. What do you think about? Are you dreaming of a different occupation? Do you picture yourself doing one special thing? What is it? Could this be your special gift? Why not try it? You may have to change direction, or get some specialized training, but if you do not follow your gifted ability and your dreams, your success will be far less than it could be. Enjoying what you are doing, and wanting to do it, is essential. Once you find what you like to do, you will be on your way. Until then you will be like a ship at sea without sails, going nowhere.

It is time for you to sit down and think very carefully. What can you do? What do you enjoy doing? What are you qualified for and would enjoy doing well? And remember, when I say qualified, I do not mean you already know how to do it. I mean, what are you really qualified to do once you have learned how? Those who try to do something they do not like or are not qualified for are not going to be successful, because they will not devote enough time to it. To make money you have to spend a lot of time and energy. Success will not come easily. In the beginning, you will have to be very hard on yourself; you must almost punish yourself. You will be making your body work harder, making your mind work overtime, and enjoying many of your old habits less. If you enjoy other activities more than your work, it will be very hard for you to achieve success. But if you can find something you enjoy doing more than your favorite pastime, then you will be successful.

Make achieving your success in life a game in which you work out the winning solution. No game has ever been invented that can offer so much fun and be so rewarding. You must train yourself to a different lifestyle and a different way of thinking. You will need to play the game every minute of every day, until you mold yourself to the life of success.

The rewards are not just monetary. You will find yourself wanting to get to work, wanting to work longer hours, thinking more and more about your work, always planning new things. For someone who has not experienced it, this may sound impossible. Yet, once you start getting this feeling, you will have a much easier time Reaching for the Gold! In fact, you won't even call it work anymore. It really becomes a challenge, a game, if you will.

You are about to enter a different world. It will be strange at first. Yes, even scary! You will have to do it alone. But don't let anyone fool you with that old saying, "It's lonely at the top." You will have people crawling over one another to reach you once you get there. And you will smile, because this terrible, hard, mean work you used to hate is suddenly fun and very rewarding.

When I look back, becoming successful has never been easy, but being poor wasn't either. And I don't think being poor has any rewards. Being successful does!

You want to make money? Okay! Before I say, "Let's do it, then!" I want to know how badly you want to make money. If you just say it, but you don't want to put anything into it, there is no way you are going to make it. You might as well stop reading this book. To make money you definitely have to have your heart set on it. You must have determination and the willingness to spend time and energy achieving it. In other words, you will have to pay your dues. You have to put something into it before you can get anything out.

Whatever you want is obtainable if you really want it and set your goal high enough. Don't expect it to come too easily or too quickly! Most people get discouraged if they don't see fast results.

Those of you who are employed may have to start your goal to riches slower than you would like. You may need to keep your present employment for the income and start your game of fun and success in the morning before work or in the evening after work. It may be in the form of on-the-job training. You may want to attend night classes, or a trade school, or study correspondence courses. It could be just working to put money aside to buy investments.

Your ideas may take years to accomplish and many extra hours to develop, but you must not get discouraged. Make it fun! Don't be afraid to get involved in something new. The most unfortunate thing that happens to a person who fears failure is that he limits himself by being afraid to try anything new. Give yourself a chance. You will not become rich overnight. You will work long, hard hours, but you will be rewarded with wealth, success, inner pride, and happiness.

Everyone has a different idea of what wealth is. You, as an individual, have to determine how much wealth you want to accumulate. The illustration I used about the limousine or the private plane should not be misleading. I am sure there are many people who would be happy if they just had a nice new car, a little fishing boat, and could take a trip once or twice a year. There is absolutely nothing wrong with that! If that is what will make you happy, then that is the goal you should set for yourself. Most of the things we are talking about in the book apply to that kind of success as well as being very wealthy. But do not set your goals lower than you really want just because you are afraid or lazy. Fear can be overcome and laziness must not be tolerated. To make this game of life fun, you must set your goals high enough to make them challenging. The bigger you dream, the higher you reach, the more interesting your game becomes.

Putting four simple words, working, dreaming, saving and investing, into action will bring you success. Don't spend foolishly. I cannot stress that enough. Don't buy on time or pay interest. I want your money to earn interest for you. Make your investments as soon as possible. Investing early will keep you from spending your money on unnecessary items. Many of you who want to be successful will not make it because you will spend your money too soon and will not want to work those extra hours.

Look around you! The people who are successful have worked very, very hard. They did not pay attention to how many hours they worked in a day. They just kept working. You will hear them say, "I worked twelve, fourteen, fifteen hours a day." And even then they didn't quit. After they went to bed, they thought and planned for the days ahead. That's why, as I said before, it is important to enjoy what you are doing.

Most of these people share a common lifestyle. They engage in some type of exercise each morning, whether jogging, or walking, or working out at a nearby gym, to help clear their minds for the busy day ahead.

They are very careful with money. They don't waste it or spend it foolishly. For every dollar you spend on unnecessary items, you will have to earn three dollars to make it up. In fact, you can never make it up. Earning money takes time and you cannot make up time.

They consider their time a valuable possession and use it wisely. Time is also important to you. Plan your days, and work carefully. When a salesperson calls on you and says, "Just listen. It won't cost you anything." Remember, it does cost you. Priorities are a must. The effective use of your time is a priority.

Always remember, you go around in life but once. Do it the best way you know how. Discipline yourself! Never take your eyes off the gold! This game of life is worth living to the fullest. You can make it happy or sad, enjoyable or depressing. You can make it what you want. Make it happy.

To know yourself you must give yourself a chance. Over fifty percent of our population, who are of working age, have never sat down long enough to find out what they would like to do. Most have never even tried to discover their natural ability. Others who know what their natural ability is have never bothered to use it. By ignoring their ability, they haven't given themselves a fair chance at success. Because of that, they will never be happy with their work, and they will never be really successful. Don't be one of those people. Get to know who you are and who you want to be. Listen to the most important person in the world, the person who knows you the best, the person who can make you happy and successful. Yes, listen to yourself.

Whatever you do in your business and personal life, do it to the utmost of your ability. If in any way you feel that what you have done could have been done better, do it over until you are happy with it. Do everything the best you can at all times.

Those in real estate and retail businesses say the three most important things are location, location, and LOCATION. In this business of success, the three most important things are Work, Motivation, and DETERMINATION! As you combine these qualities with your natural ability, you will succeed. Remember, go for excellence. Never be satisfied with less than your best. Use your natural abilities and we will see you at the top. Go for the Gold.

2

EDUCATION AND YOU

The fact is, there is too much emphasis on higher education. Many people think you have to have a degree in your chosen field to be successful. I do not believe that.

True, a person needs to prepare for success, but not necessarily by going to school. We can't all be professional people, and that is not all bad. Although degrees are not everything, they do have their advantages. If you have the qualifications for succeeding in formal education, I certainly feel you should pursue degrees in the field of your choice. But if you do not, you must not let that be an obstacle to your becoming successful and wealthy.

As you make your decision, keep in mind that most professions, such as doctors, attorneys, educators, etc., must be present on the job to earn their money. They cannot hire replacements.

People who make investments and structure their life around retail businesses, income properties and sales find it possible to spend more time away from their business and still have an income. In sales, unlike the professions, if you can find good help and train them correctly, they can be making money for you while you are away. With income properties, if you have dependable managers, they too will be making money for you when you are not there.

Your personal education for success in the business world can start at any age. The earlier you learn to work, the better off you will be. If your parents taught you the ability to work as you were growing up, you have already started your education with a worthwhile advantage.

While you were in grade school, you learned to work and acquired good work habits. If you are in high school, you should be gaining an awareness of your abilities, your likes, and your dislikes.

If you are in college or trade school, you should have your goals firmly in mind. You should be spending most of your available time on your chosen field, whether in reading or practical experience. Remember, it is education, not money, that counts at this point. Your financial rewards will come later.

During our early years in education, we are very vulnerable. We do as we are instructed to do. Throughout the years, we followed orders and suggestions, in many cases, against our will or better judgment. The trend to be a "follower" carries over into later education and influences our choosing a profession.

Young people express their rebellion in many ways: hairstyles, mode of dress, friends, music. Nearly everyone has a phase of rebellion in their lives. I don't know if I believe in all these rebellions, but if you want to rebel, do it in education. Don't let your educational system push you into classes which you don't need, understand or want, or which will only waste your time. Let me remind you, your time is very important. Put those hours to better use. Your aim is to attack your goals. Spend your hours doing that, not fulfilling someone else's dream. Once you have achieved your purpose and want to branch out into other courses for pleasurable and social interaction, that is fine. But classes that will help you fulfill your dreams should come first.

Some people can handle more classes than others. Take all the classes and get all the knowledge available for your field, but be sure you have enough time to do your best in them. Do not spread yourself so thin you do not have enough time to become Number One in your field.

Many young people go to college because their parents want them to, or because, in their social strata, it is expected of them. Higher education, that is, education beyond high school, should have a definite goal in mind. No matter what age you are, set your goals, and then study and work to fulfill those goals.

Choose your course of study because you want it and are qualified for it, not because someone else suggests it.

I almost made the big mistake of becoming a pharmacist after coming home from the war. Two factors strongly influenced my decision. First, the profession looked glamorous to me. Second, and probably the most influential, I wanted to please my parents. Fortunately for me, my chemistry background in high school had not been strong enough to prepare me for the courses I would need in college, so I dropped out. Subsequently, I made the best decision of my life. I enrolled in the business courses available and began to use my natural abilities. My interests and understanding had always been centered in the world of sales. Business was what I wanted to do, what I enjoyed. And for the first time in my life, my grades proved it. If I had become a pharmacist, my whole life would have been spent working at something for which I was not qualified, and probably would not have enjoyed. I would have always been discontented, and I never would have been as successful.

I am not suggesting you take only classes you enjoy. There may be times you will need to take certain "undesirable" classes to be the best in your field. Neither am I telling you to disregard advice from your parents, teachers, or counselors. On the contrary. Get all the advice you can, and have an open mind. But don't be led into a profession or business that does not use your gifted abilities. If that happens, you will not be content. Without contentment, you will not reach your goal. And besides, why not be happy in your work?

If you got poor grades and had a hard time in school, your parents, teachers, relatives and friends probably gave you numerous reasons why you would never succeed. Not only that, your report cards proved it. But a report card cannot see inside you and often does more harm than good. It does not grade your determination, neither does it grade how hard a worker you are. It could very easily not grade you at all on your main qualification for success: your natural ability. So don't sit back and tell yourself you are a failure.

I just want you to be good at one thing. Whatever you are best suited for, that is what I want you to work on. Work very hard until you are as good as, or better than, anyone else in your field. That is when you will succeed in life and find your happiness.

Many people dream of transforming their hobby or skill into a business but don't know where to begin. Have you considered going back to school? Your local college or university may be offering extension courses for would-be entrepreneurs.

According to statistics, many new businesses fail because the owners lack managerial and technical skills. Many potential entrepreneurs don't know how to start a business, and if they do start it, they don't know how to market it. Often the need for capital is more than expected. Courses in financing, management, pricing of products and services, structuring your business, marketing your product, advertising and promotion are all good suggestions. But always keep in mind, book-learning is one thing; practical application of that learning is the object of education.

Some colleges and universities offer chances to learn from fellow class members and case studies as well as from books. This learning plus practical application can be used to plan and develop your own business. Other studies you might want to include could be cash-flow budgeting, simple accounting, real estate and business law.

The benefits of education can be enormous to you financially. But formal education is not always the answer to your success. Work itself is a form of education. In fact, it is the best form of education you can have. If you have a good trade, you have already made use of practical education. If you don't have a trade, train for one which you will enjoy, are qualified to do, and won't mind doing.

Remember, if you are not a straight-A student or blessed with a real sharp brain, don't be discouraged! Just keep working towards your success. If you do not have the means for education or trade school, you can probably achieve just as much by working your way up in the field of your choice.

Whichever direction you choose, higher education or practical, on-the-job training, be sure you are pursuing the right career. Why not take a course in bookkeeping or business and, at the same time, start working? While you are taking these courses, use your time wisely. Start getting experience in your area of interest. Learning how to work should be your main purpose. Never be afraid to experiment or venture into the field for which you are training. Your experiment or venture will tell you one of two things: you will either be happy, or you will find it is not the right field for you.

Sometimes incidents occur which are very frightening and discouraging, but they happen for a reason. For instance, prior to the time I went to college, I worked part-time for a furniture store. My jobs were to repair furniture, help with the deliveries, and sell when the store was busy. To my surprise, my boss came up to me one day and told me that, because business was slow and sales were down, he had to let me go. It was indeed a shock! The month before he had told me what a great job I was doing. Naturally, I was very depressed, and my pride was hurt. But looking back, I see it was a blessing in disguise. If he had not fired me, there is a possibility my life could have been spent working for him as a salesperson.

There are very few people who go through life without having some disappointments. Do not let setbacks stop you. If you are a determined person, you will someday look back and find your stumbling blocks were actually stepping stones to success. They are part of your practical education. Learn from them, and use them to your advantage.

During the Great Depression, there were many people who suffered drastic financial setbacks. There was one man who took his loss, added hard work, and became a success. I would like to share his story with you.

He was an uneducated father with a family to support. He couldn't find work anywhere, but somehow he had to provide. His home was close to a heavily-traveled highway. Many hours were spent watching the traffic go by, wondering how he was going to make a living.

One day he had an idea. Why not start a hamburger stand along the side of the road? So he put up a small booth and, on a little kerosene burner, started his hamburger business. As people passed by, they saw his signs, smelled his hamburgers cooking, and stopped to try them out.

Soon his stand became a favorite place for people to stop regularly on their way to and from work. His business began to grow. Why? His hamburgers were plump and juicy. He used fresh, fluffy, fat hamburger buns. The dressings he used were the best, and he never skimped on them when serving his delicious hamburgers. Plus, he gave the best service in town. In a short while, his stand was too small to accommodate the business, and he had to expand.

Now, keep in mind that all this success was happening during the Depression, when most people had little or no money to spare, and other businesses were failing. He not only made enough money to provide for his family's needs, he was even able to send his son away to college.

While the son was away at school, he was told the economy was financially depressed. When he came home, he explained the situation to his father, and advised him to cut back on supplies and let some of his help go. Unfortunately, his father listened. He reasoned, "My son is educated. He should know. I am uneducated, so I should listen to him, or I will lose my business."

He started skimping on his meat and buns, and let some of his help go. His service got worse and worse, and the word got around. People stopped coming for his hamburgers. No longer was his "the place" to stop for lunch. Soon he was out of business. He told a friend, "My son is very smart. He was right. There is a Depression, and he predicted my business would fail."

In his uneducated status, he saw a need and he filled it. Because he used his natural ability to fulfill his dream, he became a success. But by following negative, "educated" advice, he lost all the years of hard work he had put into his dream. He again sat on his porch, watching the traffic go by. But now his situation was worse than before. He was now convinced that because of his lack of education, he could never become successful.

I hope you see the reason for this story. There are times when you are better off using your own judgment. Some people put too much emphasis on believing in other people. Don't let this kind of tragedy happen to you. Education, or the lack of it, does not determine your success. It is only the amount of work you are willing to put into your dreams, and your belief in yourself, that can make your dreams come true.

Some people are always educating themselves, preparing themselves for one career after another, but never making a final decision. They remind me of ships at sea without rudders, unable to go in any specific direction. It's okay to be cautious when making career decisions, but sometime you must make that decision. You have to jump in, take your chances, and use the knowledge and education you have been acquiring. Put it to practical use. Don't be like a farmer who gets up and harnesses his horse every morning, but never uses the horse.

These people feel secure while educating themselves, but unless they put their education to practical use, it will never give them financial satisfaction. Plus they rob themselves of the chance for self-fulfillment. Your purpose in life is to achieve goals, rather than just exist. Each morning, when you get up, determine to do something which will make your life worthwhile. If you have taken time to educate yourself, use that education, and the security you experienced in preparing yourself will be translated into security in your accomplishments.

By now you must realize I do not believe that someone must go

15

through college and get degrees to become successful. But I do believe that in your journey through life to success and riches, your education never ends. Life itself is a continuing education. Educating yourself goes on forever, even after you have started your business and are successful.

It is always good to take classes in other areas that can expand your success. Success is determined by how many hats you are willing to try on, and how many of those hats will fit you well. You must educate yourself in as many fields as possible, so you can effectively evaluate your situation. Your goal may not necessarily be the acquiring of diplomas or licenses, but a general working knowledge, so you can make your own sound decision.

You are probably thinking, "You want me to work twelve hours a day, and then you want me to take some classes, too?" And my answer is, I never promised becoming wealthy would be easy. I never said, and never will say, that you won't spend many hours achieving success. I will tell you over and over again, you are going to work hard for it. If you are worried about losing sleep at night, keep in mind that most adults really only need five or six hours of sleep.

Do not think that reading this book, or making up your mind, will make you wealthy. Becoming wealthy is not easy, and no one has ever accomplished it while sitting around doing nothing. You will earn every dollar you make. It will be a long hard struggle, involving many hours of work, study, and preparation.

But won't you have fun!

3

MAN AGAINST HIMSELF

Most of us work against ourselves. If we can overcome this handicap, nothing can hinder us from attaining the gold. A handicap can be just imaginary. It can be fearfulness. The fear of venturing out, fear of trying something new. In many cases, it is a fear of just trying. Remember the old saying, nothing ventured, nothing gained? There is a lot of truth in that statement.

Do you feel you are struggling with a handicap? In what way? Do you have an emotional problem? Do you feel handicapped because you are an unwed parent or divorcee struggling to raise a family? Are you physically handicapped? You may find you are able to succeed in areas where others cannot. A handicap only becomes a hinderance to your progress when you permit it to be. It is okay for others to feel sorry for you, but you should never waste energy feeling sorry for yourself. Just keep in mind, nearly everyone has a handicap. Obviously, some are more noticeable than others. But no matter what your handicap is, it should not hinder your success, if it is accepted and dealt with openly.

Your physical or emotional handicap does not eliminate your gifted ability. In fact, your gift may be enhanced because of your handicap. When someone has a handicap, their body and mind develop a counter-reaction to overcome that handicap. This counter-reaction may actually be your gifted ability. If you use it to your benefit, it could make you more gifted than the next person. It might possibly be your key to success. So find your gift and use it. You may have to work harder to accomplish your goal, but because you are used to struggling, you will not quit. Remember, no one can do everything. Doing what you can to the best of your ability will bring you that success.

17

The other day I saw a waiter with a crippled arm. Through practice he had learned to position and manipulate his arm so that his condition was barely noticeable. His smile was big, his demeanor was pleasant, and he was enjoying what he was doing. He could have used his disability as an excuse for not doing that type of work because it "required two good arms", but he didn't. He accepted his disability and worked with it. If he keeps this attitude, he will succeed, because he is not letting a physical factor interfere with his progress. By keeping the same determination he is now using, he will reach the gold.

When I came out of military service, I had an eighty percent hearing loss. My social life became limited because I couldn't hear what was being said around me. My lack of hearing was a real problem. I could have sat back and pitied myself, but instead I went to school and learned to lip read. There were many times I didn't hear what was going on around me, but I didn't let myself get discouraged. Through the years I have used my nearly silent world to strengthen my powers of concentration. I have the ability to think better, to day-dream better, and to plan better. I found the advantage of my disability, used it accordingly, and never let it stand in the way of my success. I made it work for me. You can do the same.

Some people only <u>feel</u> they have a handicap. For example, consider the person who has a big nose. That person feels self-conscious and imagines everyone is always staring at their big nose, rather than really seeing the whole person. With their own attention centered on their nose, they probably have never taken time to consider their positive qualities. Maybe their eyes are beautiful, or their personality is so great that others don't even notice their nose.

If you are, or feel you are, handicapped, find the areas where your abilities and interests coincide. Then use those abilities and interests to compensate for your deficit. It is self-defeating to sit back and excuse yourself by saying you can't do what other people can do. Do not defeat yourself. You can do just as much as you want to do.

Often being a single parent is a handicap. Every morning you wonder who you are today. Am I mother? Father? Provider? Care-giver? One of the first emotional reactions, if your mate leaves, is the feeling of failure. You may want to hide in that feeling, convincing yourself you cannot succeed in anything. Doing this will keep you from using your abilities. As a single parent, you have to wear different hats at different times. But if you can learn to use the knowledge you gain while wearing those hats to help you progress in your daily life and emotional growth, you are well on your way up that mountain of success. In fact, you have reached an important plateau in your development.

Conquering an emotional handicap begins with accepting it. Many single parents or divorcees are emotionally handicapped but try to hide their feelings. You will cope with your problem better if you admit it. I know of one single parent who thought everyone knew she was an unwed mother. She spent most of her energy looking at other people enviously, assuming their situation was so much better than hers. She was emotionally blinded, handicapped by her situation. Looking at other people and wishing you were them will not solve your problem. You must begin to accept yourself where you are and concentrate on what you can be. To dream of the person you would like to be is to waste the person you are.

If you are an unwed mother, divorcee, or a man or woman alone, one problem you may face is a reluctance to apply yourself to anything meaningful for any length of time. Are you afraid of failing? Do you allow yourself to advance to a certain point, and then permit your fear of failure to frighten you into inactivity when the opportunity to venture out presents itself? If so, you have allowed your experience of failure to become an obstruction which hinders you trying anything again. Don't let this feeling of failure in your personal life keep you from attaining financial success or enjoying the rest of your personal life. Your situation may actually be a blessing in disguise. Some people find themselves single and realize they finally have a chance to succeed on their own, and become excited about it.

Often parents hide in the fact that they need to be taking care of their children, so they choose not to work. By starting a business in your home, you have very little overhead, and your work place is near. Your children do need to be taken care of, but you need to take care of yourself as well.   Statistics show that women are going into business at one and a half times the rate of men. It is also projected that forty percent of all self-employed individuals will be women by the end of the century. Working at home can be very appealing, as it allows room for independence and extra income, while giving ample time for home responsibilities.

If you have children and want to go to school, there are many programs sponsored by the government which can make that possible. Community colleges and universities often provide day-care facilities for parents who are attending classes. If finances are a problem, there are many financial aid programs available through your local educational institution which can eliminate a large portion of your tuition.

If you are physically disabled and can't get out, you can still work. The trend today is to set up home businesses which do typing, bookkeeping, and many other services for local businesses which do not have a need for full time employees. Why not get some training, decide what services you want to offer, and open your own business?

According to recent statistics, there are 23,000,000 people who work full or part-time from their homes. This is definitely the age of the home-centered business. The government projects that by the year 2000, more than one-third of our nation's work force will be working from their homes in either a full or part-time capacity. You could become a part of this growing segment of society and establish an office in your home. Then you can work at home, tailoring your work and your abilities to your liking.

If you want to go out and work rather than start a business but can't work eight hours a day, the fact that many businesses prefer hiring part-time help provides a golden opportunity for you. Train or retrain yourself for what you would like to do and are capable of doing, then find a part-time job in that field.

Working part-time can be advantageous. Money alone is not the important factor here. Your employment can be a means of getting out of that tunnel, so you can start climbing your mountain. Being in the work force will offer you new horizons and give direction to your life. You will have the opportunity to train yourself for the field you would like to enter full-time, possibly after your children are grown, either working for someone else or starting your own business. You can acquire knowledge about and insight into investing, and equip yourself to earn sufficient money to make those investments.

If you are looking for work, here are some things you need to do:

1. Send out resumes
2. Talk to as many people as possible
3. Answer ads in the paper
4. Study for the type of work you want and enjoy
5. Work on answers for your interview

6. Look for a business that needs your expertise
7. Check with unemployment agencies

Sometimes finding a position is not easy. Finding the right job is even harder, and no job is perfect. To help you determine what type of work will make your employment enjoyable, there are some vital questions you must answer when considering a job opportunity. Go through the following list and answer each one yes or no. Be honest. The only one you have to answer to is you.

Will you be happy?
Will it help you create your natural ability?
Is the salary sufficient?
Does the job involve selling?
Will you work on commission?
Will you be responsible for training or supervision?
Will it give you personal pride and growth?
Will you be helping others improve their lives?
Will this job allow you to be creative?
Can you learn new skills on the job?
Are your hours flexible?
Is it hands-on work?
Will this job provide 'job security'?
Is promotion possible?
Will you work independently?
Will you be encouraged to take on more responsibility?
Will you be communicating with others constantly?
Is the atmosphere friendly?
Is individual achievement recognized?
Do you have far to commute?
If travel is involved, will you have to be away from home often?
Does the position offer good benefits?
(Plus any others you may think of)

Now, go back through the list again and mark an "x" beside each quality you desire in a position.

Consider these questions and your answers carefully. By studying your "yes" answers as well as the questions you have marked with an "x", you are now more equipped to decide whether the job you are considering is the type of employment you want.

The process is the same whether you are looking for full- or part-time employment. You may feel the inner look is unimportant, especially if you only want part-time work, but if you pay close attention to what you are telling yourself, your search for satisfying employment will be much more rewarding.

Unless you are very lucky, it will take much work and preparation, plus you will experience many hours of waiting and frustration. Job hunting can be very humiliating, even to the point of wanting to give up. But you must not give up. This life we live in was not meant to be easy and when you are looking for a position, it seems employers are out there to prove it. You will wonder why someone won't stop what they are doing just long enough to listen to you and help.

The difficulties you face may be to prepare you for all the bumps you will encounter on your way to the top. You will have to take the attitude these frustrations are some of the dues you pay for success. They are good forerunners, or they can be terrible stumbling blocks. It is a test to find out who is capable and worthy of success, who has the ability to succeed. It is up to you, the individual, to use them as stepping stones for your success.

As you can see, this is an important time of your life. So, prepare yourself, and don't take no for an answer. You can and must do it. The rewards later make all the struggle worthwhile.

While you are working, continually prepare yourself for other ventures. Because you are using one ability does not mean you should sit back in the evening and watch television. The majority of our population spends too many hours doing just that. It is fine to relax once in a while, but you should constantly be alert for new opportunities. What a shame to waste all those hours, when you could be dreaming, planning and creating your own life. Don't waste your life away watching other people's success stories. Look for new ideas. When you find one you would like to try, put on another hat. You would be surprised how much fun it is to have two, three, four or more different areas of interest. It is more exciting and rewarding to create and live your own personal success story.

You can become anything you want to be, but you have to make that decision. Don't let your age, friends, or your mental outlook keep you from reaching out to the future and going on with your life.

Success is for you. If you say it can't happen to you, you are defeating yourself. Many of today's successful people were in your situation at one time or another. If circumstances are not falling together for you the way you would like and you feel depressed, don't quit trying. Remember, no one starts at the top, and reaching the top never comes easy. Everyone learns to crawl before they learn to walk, and you have to be able to walk before you can run. The same is true as you work towards your financial success. Take one plateau at a time. Don't look back. Be determined to do what is necessary to achieve your success, and one day you will find yourself at the top.

In conclusion, there is an old saying, "If life gives you a lemon, make lemonade." I would like you to make your own lemonade, just the way you like it.

4

DAYDREAMING

Daydreaming is the art of taking yourself from where you are and putting yourself where you would like to be. It doesn't hurt to daydream to make your dreams come true.

Sometimes daydreaming is daydreaming; sometimes it is planning. In this game of success, daydreaming is the most fun, exciting, and relaxing pastime an entrepreneur can enjoy. Undoubtedly, it is one of the most important parts of the game. It is also very convenient. You can daydream while driving your car, sitting in your office, or relaxing in your living room.

I did most of my dreaming after going to bed at night, sometimes lying awake for hours, dreaming and planning my future success. Daydreaming was very important in structuring my life, planning my business, and determining my investment strategies. I was always amazed at the new ideas which were spawned during those quiet times. I still am.

In everyday life you have to be realistic. When you daydream, you can let your wildest imaginings appear before your eyes in living color. Even though your daydreaming and planning are two different things, they are closely related. Your dreams can be harnessed and used as a basis for your plans. I have been dreaming the same type of dream since I was a young man. I always start out trying to achieve success. My dreams never quite seem to reach a climax, and my success never comes easily, because I always picture myself investing the money I am making in order to make more money. At the end of my dreams, I am always more successful than when I started, but not as successful as I would like to be. I am still struggling, still trying to reach a goal, getting ready to try on another hat.

Many hours were spent thinking about the business I was in, or

24

dreaming about a business I would like to get into later. Then I would plan and work towards the fulfillment of that dream. My dream couldn't always be accomplished that month, or even that year, but I aimed my life in that direction. Admittedly, dreams do change. In fact, they change quite often. But as your aims and goals change in accordance with your dreams, it is thrilling to watch it all come true.

In my dreams, I always planned for the next morning, the next week, the next month, the next year, and for the rest of my life. Because I was consistent in dreaming and then working to make those dreams come true, my life has turned out very much as I dreamed it would be. Living the dream is even more fun than dreaming it.

If you will take the time to dream, beginning now, right where you are in your life, and then work hard to make those dreams come true, you will find as much enjoyment in daydreaming and accomplishing as I find. You need not wait until you have large sums of money on hand before you start to dream. You should constantly be dreaming, accumulating and expanding. Your plans, dreams and thoughts actually do correspond with how you are going to succeed. Dream now with what you have! It costs nothing to dream, and it often pays big dividends.

Daydreaming is more enjoyable than watching television. You can create your own story, write your own script, choose your own characters, be the director, and even star in the show all at the same time. Unlike television, you can make your story come out right every time.

Daydreams are not just relaxing, and they are not dreams you think of and then forget. These daydreams are essential. You need your dreams to keep you interested. Your dreams should not be dreams you let slip away from you, but actually plans of what you want to accomplish in your lifetime. They should be a stimulus, getting you ready for the next day, week, month, or year. They are guidelines for your accomplishments. Letting your mind be free to wander through all possibilities is essential, but dream a plan you can fulfill. Then be willing to work hard to do just that.

Many people daydream but never do anything about their dreams. That is absolutely the opposite of what you should do. To avoid misleading you, let's call your dreams "plans." In fact, let's call them "dream-plans." I do not want you to dream your life away. But in order to succeed, you have to have a dream-plan for your future. It may not work out exactly the way you dreamed it originally, but you must have a goal, a plan to work on. That is what daydreaming is all about.

My first taste of success, the kind of success where you build a business into something special, came when I owned the grocery business in North Dakota. During those seven years, I was constantly dreaming bigger and better dreams that I wanted to fulfill, while I was building my business.

My plans were structured around my dream of eventually moving to California and investing there. When the time was right, I sold my business for a good profit by midwest standards. Upon reaching California, I soon realized my profits were only worth about half as much as I thought they would be. Although this was quite a shock, I did not let it destroy my dream. I knew I had made the right decision. I kept looking for the right investment, and I went right on dreaming.

I spent many hours, even days, traveling up and down California, criss-crossing the state, trying to find something to fit my dreams. One thing for sure, the longer you look, the harder it becomes to make up your mind, and the more frustrated you become. I would much rather work at building a business than try to find one to purchase. There were times when I thought it would be easier to simply get a job and go to work, but I didn't want to destroy my dream.

Poring over all the newspapers I could get hold of filled my evenings. I called realtors all over the state. I knew I was spending my hard-earned money looking for my dream, and reality was pressing in on me. I had to get settled somewhere soon and register my four children in school. Necessity forced me into getting my California real estate license and going to work. Finding my dream was going to take longer than I thought, but I was determined to keep on looking.

Upon returning to Sacramento for the third time, I purchased a home and went to work for a Sacramento real estate firm. I never gave up on my dreams, and finally, one day, after nearly two years of searching, I found it.

In a town about 90 miles north of Sacramento, I found a small mobile home park, purchased it, and went to work for myself. I continued selling real estate in a nearby town, but soon decided I wasn't getting ahead fast enough.

One day while daydreaming, it occurred to me to go into selling mobile homes. It was a new trend which should catch on quickly because it was good, cheap housing. If I sold only one mobile home a month and netted a thousand dollars profit per unit, (doing all the set-up work and all the bookkeeping to eliminate extra expense), I would be better off than I was selling real estate. My dream was to expand the business from there.

So there I was again, starting something I knew absolutely nothing about. It meant purchasing a sales license, obtaining permits to operate a sales lot in the front of my little park, and getting myself ready to sell something I had never sold before. After I acquired all my permits and licenses, the hardest part was finding a mobile home manufacturing company that would sell me one mobile home at a time. Those steps alone took me months of hard work and planning.

I was determined to do the work myself and keep the profit. Keep in mind that I knew nothing about setting up a mobile home, which not only included blocking, but also plumbing, electrical work, and any necessary repairs. I didn't want to hire the work out, so I had to learn it all from scratch. Hiring set-up crews, repair men, sales personnel and a bookkeeper would have caused me to lose most of my income. As a result, my chance for success would have been unlikely, or at least hampered.

By purchasing a mobile home, displaying it at the front of my little trailer park and selling it within the month, one segment of my dream was fulfilled and I made a thousand dollars. With the extra money from that sale and the small income from the park, my dream was beginning to become a reality. I tried it again, and again I sold the mobile home. After a few months of success, I decided if I could sell one a month, I could surely sell two. I started selling two mobile homes a month, and then three. My sales kept increasing until eventually I became one of the largest mobile home dealers in Northern California.

Along with the increase in business came the realization that mobile home buyers needed mobile home insurance. Obviously, there had to be good money in that, so I started studying insurance, and got my license to sell. This also proved profitable. I had found another need and met it. This is what I meant when I said in Chapter Two that you should be continuously educating yourself. How much easier it would have been for me not to study for my insurance exam, and let someone else sell the insurance. But preparing myself, and wearing that extra hat, was another stepping stone up that mountain of success.

I wonder how many of you reading this book will actually dream and work at your dreams. Those who do not will have only limited success, but those of you who do will find success.

When the corner property across the street from my little park became available, I purchased it with a down payment I could afford and committed myself to years of payments. Even though the street at that time was only two lanes, I had enough foresight to see that the land would someday be valuable. By now I knew my mobile home sales business was going to be a success, and I welcomed the opportunity to expand. Another dream was now fulfilled. I could expand my sales lot while the property went up in value.

But success didn't stop my dreaming. The next dream was to build my own mobile home park.

Although I do not want to go into the building of the park in detail, there are areas in that part of my life which might be of interest and may initiate some new ideas for you.

Many times, while trying to acquire the land and the necessary permits to build the mobile home park, I could have become very discouraged and quit. It took approximately three years from the time I decided to go ahead on the park until it was completed. Nearly every day during those three years I encountered nothing but discouragement. One problem after another! Problems with the county, or state, or engineer, or the price of the land loomed in front of me. The problems went on and on.

Two or three days a week were spent trying to purchase the land which I thought was suitable. The seller was asking a price which was too high for a mobile home park. I had my figures and finally, after much determination, I purchased the property for what I thought it was worth.

I also worked very closely with my engineer drawing the plans. After the plans were completed, I spent many evening hours going over them at home, then sat down the next day with him to make any necessary changes. Obtaining county and state approval dragged on for months and involved many changes. Acquiring county approval was the most difficult. There were neighbors who weren't sure about the mobile home park, so they questioned it. Hearings were held, at which time I had to explain in detail what I had in mind, realizing the neighbors' complaints could stop the construction of the park.

Meanwhile, I was spending many hours with my bank, obtaining the financing I wanted at the lowest rate possible. In the end, my persistence paid off. I obtained my financing at a good rate of interest and saved myself thousands of dollars.

Admittedly, it was discouraging at times, and it was very hard work, but building that park was one of my best investments. If I had been a weaker person and not so determined, I could have lost that golden opportunity. I have shared this story with you to give you some idea of what can be done if you dare to dream big enough, and then set your mind to work hard enough to make it all come true. Be prepared for a lot of hard work and many frustrating hours. Do not give up, and in the end you will find that all the effort used in Reaching for the Gold is worthwhile. Many people will give up on an idea if it becomes too difficult. So consequently, for those who don't give up, the idea becomes a better investment. The harder it is to acquire something, the better it pays off in the end.

Picture yourself as a mountain climber. Visualize a high rugged mountain in front of you. Climbing to the top of that mountain will take determination. Before you even start to climb, you must plan your strategy. In your planning you must visualize obstacles you may meet as you journey upward. You will not reach the top in a day. As you climb, you will reach one plateau after another. It is the same with the game of success.

A mountain climber who stops climbing will never reach the summit of a mountain. You will have to have the same kind of determination as a successful climber. Each dream is another plateau in your life which you must work to reach. To succeed, you must be forever climbing. Keep reaching towards the peak of your success. Once you have reached the first plateau, look it over, set your eyes on the next plateau, and plan how you are going to get there. Keep climbing from plateau to plateau, until you have reached your goals and fulfilled your dreams.

It is possible you can do it in your present position. If you are in a field you enjoy and are just starting your dream, find out what types of training will bring your advancement. Most companies look for people who are willing to work hard to get ahead, and are willing to put in extra hours for training in order to accomplish it. If you are happy and content where you are, stay there, and fulfill your dream.

Follow the same guidelines; work hard, budget yourself, keep a good credit rating, avoid paying interest and invest wisely. As your investments start paying off, use that money to reinvest. Make your money work for you.

If the company you are with offers no chance for advancement, I suggest looking elsewhere, either for a similar line of work or a new field which interests you. Or, why not start your own business? The reason I suggest starting your own business is if you are a creative person and a hard worker with big dreams, then owning your own business should be better for you than working for someone else. Once you make up your mind, put all your effort into making it succeed. Never let your dreams be stifled by inactivity or lack of energy! Don't let setbacks scare you or disillusion you. Make up your mind you will have problems. Be prepared for them and be certain you can come out on top. Once you have your plan and your dream, don't let anyone or anything keep you from achieving it.

Possibly you are in a certain line of work only because it was the only thing you could find at the moment. If this is the case, but your dreams are elsewhere, go find your dream! By all means, do not limit your success. The peak of the mountain is your limit. Don't set your sights any lower.

Maybe you have a brand new idea or have an invention which you would like to market. Do some experimentation with your idea. Try it!. Teach yourself by trial and error! What would have happened to the Wright brothers' flying machine if they had never dared to try their idea? Possibly it would still be sitting on the drawing board. Obviously, someone else would have discovered how to make men fly, and the Wright brothers would have missed the opportunity to give the world an invention of limitless value. Your invention or idea could change the world. But you will never know unless you try it. Don't wait until someone else comes up with the idea, and then say you thought of it a long time ago, but didn't really think it would work. Dream it, then make it work, for you!

While you are striving to succeed, I want you to practice the art of dream-planning. It is a good idea to keep a note pad handy. Or you may find it more convenient to use a small recorder to record your thoughts. No matter how you do it, it is a must! Ideas and dreams never come exactly the same twice. You may forget the idea all together, or you may forget the most important part of the idea, the one that will bring you success. Organizing your thinking, as well as your lifestyle, is just as important as going from one plateau to another on your journey to the top. Keeping track of your ideas and plans will help do both for you.

You must always plan ahead before you even attempt to start a business. You will need to continue planning while your business is going and growing. Your plans must always be subject to change. You will have to plan your inventory, if you are in sales. You will have to plan your advertising and promotion. You will have to plan what types of service you will give your customers, if that is your type of business. If you are in real estate, you will have to determine which field is best for you, and then you must be willing to put many hours into it to make it work. If you are manufacturing a product, you will have to plan a quality control system that is better than the next person's in order to get a corner on the market. If you have an invention, you must plan and dream how you can make it, package it, market it, sell it, and make a profit.

As you dream-plan, you will be constantly working, trying to catch up with the dreams you had the day before. Just when you think you have caught up, you will create another plateau, dream and challenge to reach towards. It becomes a daily struggle trying to keep up with your dreams.

You should also be planning your investments, even your retirement. A successful person plans all the time. Good planning makes good sense and a successful lifestyle. Even after you have become successful, you will want to continue using your habitual daydreaming, as you enjoy your retirement and plan for future investments. Success never lies still! If it is allowed to do so, it will become like a stagnant pond. Your dreams will keep your quest for success fresh and moving like a rushing mountain stream.

Daydreaming is one of the most vital ingredients of becoming successful. To be a success, you must dream of success. You must picture yourself at the top and have enough confidence in yourself to get there. The simple fact is, anyone can make it. Once you are dreaming of success, you must break it down step by step. Then, working step by step, you must make it come true. This planning will take many hours of concentration, preparation and work. But it can and should be fun! You cannot reach for the gold and accomplish your success in an eight-hour day. In fact, you can't really box success into any certain number of hours. Working at something that interests you is one key to success. Another is keeping yourself so busy you don't have time to spend your money.

Success is essential to me. In my daydreaming, I always reach for more, want to achieve more, and after achieving that, still want more! It is this attitude which keeps me dreaming today. I am always working to accomplish the dreams of the day before. I prosper, but I'm never quite satisfied. Whenever I accomplish one goal, I use what I have gained to bring another daydream into reality. I am constantly struggling. I never feel I have reached all the plateaus I was meant to reach. My dreams push me onward, forever onward. Each time I am about to have a dream-plan fulfilled and contemplate sitting back to relax, I set myself a new goal and struggle again to reach that next plateau. You will have to discipline yourself with the same tactics. I would never be happy without goals or dreams, and neither should you.

Dream of what you would like to do. Dream of the person you would like to be and the clothes you would like to wear. Dream of what you would like to have: what kind of automobile, what sort of business, how much income. Dream about anything and everything! What would make you smile? What would make you happy? How much money would you like to have? What kind of home would you like to live in? What sort of office would you like? What kind of trips would you like to take? Would you like to have a second or third home? Would you like to play golf or take a cruise? What other investments would you like to make? What other dreams would you like to accomplish?

Everyone has different desires, so I can't tell you what kind of dreams to dream! You must determine your own dreams, and then you must dream them for yourself. And with each dream, set yourself a plateau. The height of your plateau is important. If you set your plateau too low, you will not accomplish much because you won't be expecting much from yourself. If you set yourself a high plateau, similar to climbing Mount Everest, you are going to accomplish much. You may never reach the peak, but you are bound to reach many plateaus in your trying. Even if you only reach a couple of plateaus above where you are right now, wouldn't it be worth the effort?

Dream-planning is so important I want you to lay the book aside right now, go someplace where it is comfortable and quiet, and take some time to dream. Picture yourself successful, fulfilling your dreams.

Welcome back! Now that you have fulfilled your dreams in your imagination and have pictured yourself as successful, you must go out and do the same in reality. Sit down with yourself and create a plan. You need a plan for right now, a plan for five years from now, and a plan for later on in life. These plans should all coincide with one another. I do not mean you have to plan your whole life today. That is impossible. At the same time, the importance of starting some-where must not be overlooked. The best time and place to start planning, acting, and working to fulfill your dream-plan is right now. Every day will bring new circumstances, and your dreams will have to change, but you will have set yourself some goals.

Remember, you only have so many hours in a lifetime to spend on this game of success. When you are young, it seems like a tremendous amount of time, but as you grow older you will wonder where the time went and why you wasted so much of it. Everything you do now influences your life later on. If you don't get in the habit of planning your time and dreaming your dreams correctly in order to bring success, you may find it necessary to start over in the middle of the stream. This can be disastrous. Every hour you spend foolishly trying to attain or accomplish something you do not need is wasted time.

In conclusion, the goal of this chapter is to inspire you to dream of riches and happiness, plan for riches and happiness, and work for riches and happiness, from one plateau to the next, until you reach the top. Your dream-plans are extremely important. Don't take them lightly. Trying to reach for the gold without a dream or a plan is like trying to cross the country without a road map.

No matter what game you are playing, whether it is the Olym-pics, business, investments, or even your personal life, if you are determined to win, you have to work towards that goal and earn the right to make that winning yours.

Dream of the gold, not the bronze. Your dreams are really your plans, and they may be your life. You can either have your dreams come true, or you can let them slip by. It is up to you. If you make them come true, then your dreams really are your plans! If you let them slip by unfulfilled, then they are no more than dreams.

Only you can fulfill your dreams. To fulfill your dreams you must live them, work at them, and keep climbing until they are a reality. Have an exciting journey as you climb the mountain of success, using your dream-plans as your motivation. There is a golden horizon waiting for you at the top.

Happy dreaming.

5

FACING SOME FACTS

I would like to give you something to think about. Within their first year, eighty percent of new businesses fail. Of the remaining twenty percent, a large number will fail in their second, third, fourth, or fifth year. Your chances of success are not very good. Those of you who are determined to plan and to watch your business are going to be in that twenty percent bracket. Those of you who think you can let your business run itself are going to be in the eighty percent bracket. If you do not have the desire to do what is absolutely necessary to run a good business, you are better off not even planning to start one.

I have not told you this to discourage you, but to warn you that running a business takes a lot of planning and work. Many people who start a new business immediately think they are important. They think they have to go out spending money to impress people, go out for coffee, or spend hours having lunch, even to the point of having cocktails, while their help is trying to run their business. How can that work? If you are not interested in your business, your help will not be interested in it either. You are very wrong to think you can open a business but not pay attention to it. It can only fail! If you plan your business seriously, pay attention to it, spend your money wisely, and avoid depending on your help to run your business, you will be in the top twenty percent and stay in that winning position.

If you are determined enough to become successful, it can happen. I must caution you again, you will never achieve success by acting important. Your business hours need to be kept for working. Set a good example for your help.

Now, you may be saying, "I could never succeed in starting a business. I don't feel I am capable enough or know enough about business. And besides that, I don't have enough money." These are only excuses. What you feel is fear and insecurity. If you make up your mind what to do, you will find you really are capable, and there really is a way. The simple fact that you are reading this book tells me you have the will to succeed.

Before you start to work, though, you must determine your objectives and goals, and you must think them through carefully.

What are objectives?

Think of objectives as your model plan, what you want to accomplish through your business. For instance, if your objective is to give services in one distinct area, or to one particular age group, your objectives must determine how you will go about reaching those who need your services. What type of advertising will reach the most people in that area or age group? What sort of program will you present? How much will you need to charge? What type of surroundings do you want to create? Where should you locate your business? But the most important question your objectives must answer is whether your business will meet an apparent need in your area, or will your effort be a waste of time, energy and finances. What I am getting at is this: if you don't plan your business carefully ahead of time, you may neglect details which are essential to your success.

Once your business is started, you will need to create new objectives. How long before you want to expand? Do you want to grow quickly or slowly? How large do you want your business to be ten years from now? Do you want to hire employees? Full-time or part-time? Daily you must ask yourself the question, "Am I reaching my objectives?"

Objectives should be accomplished.

Goals should not!

Goals are the personal aims you want to accomplish in life. They keep your thoughts and activities motivated. Goals should not be accomplished, because once you have reached them you have nothing more to work towards. Keeping your goals high enough and far enough out of reach will secure in your mind the excitement of success. In contrast, if you haven't reached your goals, you must take the time to figure out why!

It may sound as though I am talking in riddles. First I tell you to make your goals so high you can't reach them, and then I tell you to figure out why you didn't. Actually, all I am telling you is that you have to keep your goals in front of you. There must always be a new goal out there which you are determined to reach.

Goals which are not reached are the motivations that get you out of bed in the morning. Without them your life and work will become complacent and boring. You will fumble around, not knowing what you want to achieve. Having goals makes you anxious, excited, even eager to get on with your day. The pleasure and enthusiasm generated each day makes your striving worthwhile, and you soon find yourself on another plateau.

Write down your new goals, along with your plan to make them work. Do not depend on just thinking about a plan. The first reason is that the idea may slip out of your mind. The second is that a plan always seems simple when it is a thought. Putting that plan into writing will help you work out obvious snags before you put it into action. Thirdly, new ideas will be generated, thereby making your original idea work even better.

Remember this. Becoming successful is not easy, but it is possible and can be fun! You must have enormous energy, mountains of patience, hours of determination, and consistent planning. Then you will experience the reward of personal satisfaction in doing something well.

PART II

FIVE KEYS TO SUCCESS

6

BUILDING UP YOUR SELF-CONFIDENCE

You may be asking the question, "How can I build up my own self-confidence to promote my success?"

It is very important that you believe in yourself and your project, whatever it is. Unless you believe in yourself, and put your mind, your soul, and your body, totally into everything you do, the rewards you attain in life will be far below your possibilities. Believe in yourself and make it work. It may not work the first time. (It very seldom does.) But that's what is fun. Fun in succeeding is to run into problems, face them head-on, figure them out, and never give up. Keep after success. If your problems knock you down, get up and try again. If they knock you down again, get up and start AGAIN!

The biggest reason most people do not start their own business is they are just plain scared. I have met people who have made good money for their employers and could have done the same for themselves, but they did not have the courage to take that first step. Most people, because they are unsure of themselves and fear failure, do not want to "rock the boat."

I also know people who work very hard but need someone to control their time, their money, and their lives, even to the point of telling them when to come to work and when to go home.

This need for outside influence reverts back to their childhood, when parents or teachers told them what to do, when to go to school, when to study, when to go home, and so on. Previously we considered the influence of report cards. In many cases, the recollection of report cards is discouraging rather than encouraging. If you are one of these people, leave those childhood influences and disappointments of your school days behind you. Begin to build up your self-confidence. Prove to yourself that you are really capable. Get rid of that negative attitude. Think nothing but positive thoughts.

We humans have a great supply of energy and should not be afraid to use it. We should not be afraid of ourselves. It is a shame to sit around and do nothing. Most people who sit around and do nothing are afraid of failure. They sit, losing time, because of fear. The most unfortunate thing that happens to a person who fears failure is that he limits himself by becoming afraid to try anything new.

Don't be afraid of failure. Everyone fails. It's just another learning process in life. How you treat that failure is what is important. Don't give up just because you fail now and then. It will happen! Learn from it. Learn all you can about why you failed, but don't let your failure stop you.

In this game of success you must learn to make more correct decisions than wrong ones. Look at the game of Monopoly (R). During the game, you move your marker 'round and 'round the board. Sometimes you stop on nothing but trouble, sometimes you "Go to Jail," but you keep playing the game, and at the end, if you make more right moves than wrong ones, you come out ahead.

It is the same in real life. If you play the game long enough and hard enough, making more right decisions than wrong ones, you will come out ahead. That's part of the game plan.

You really shouldn't care what other people think is best for you at this point in the game. Get yourself to think independently. Get away from feeling you need someone to tell you what to do, someone to control your thoughts, your time, or your ideas. Start thinking of yourself as a capable and strong person. In order to be a winner, you must be convinced you can become one.

You are always going to need people to assist you, such as bankers, CPA's, attorneys, friends, the people you purchase your merchandise from, and most of all, your customers. This help is essential. Government assistance is not.

If your surroundings make you feel you need financial assistance in order to fit in, then you may have to move away from your area and friends. You may need to make a completely new start. As long as you are around negative people, you cannot succeed. You are better off leaving all that behind you and starting over, by saying, "I will succeed, because it will make me feel good about myself." Trying to succeed will give you a better attitude about life.

In order to succeed you must be persistent as well as confident.

Persistence and confidence, not intelligence, will bring you success. Your venture has to be more important than anything else you do. Remember, the product or service you are selling is actually you. Your name is on the package. You must realize that not everyone will like your ideas. Neither will everyone need your wares. But that cannot and should not discourage you.

This game you are about to play is very close to a game of punishment. You will constantly be setting goals you can never quite reach, making money you cannot spend, and making investments on which you have to make payments. Plus you will be preparing yourself for new ventures and opportunities. You will be trying to stay on top of everything, You cannot do all this in a casual way, for you must do it as well as, or better than, anyone else. It may sound like all punishment, but it is actually very rewarding.

There will be times when you want to give up, when you can't see how you are going to succeed, when you feel everything you do falls apart. From the time you begin your education to the point in your life when you have money to invest, you must prepare and expect setbacks. These periods in your life will be crucial. You should be strong enough to overcome them and accept them as part of your education. Never let them get you down. They should make you more determined than ever to succeed. How you react to them will have great bearing on your future success. Never take them lightly.

Many millionaires became wealthy because they had dreams, and they made their dreams come true. Maybe you have a dream. Maybe you have already tried to succeed at various types of businesses and have always seemed to fail, at least in your own eyes. Maybe, in the eyes of those whom you influence most, you are really quite successful and talented.

I want to share with you a new approach to your view of your failures. Try looking at them like this. You jumped headlong into something new and exciting with all your energy, and then failed when you wanted so much to succeed. You feel you made a fool of yourself. You may think you would have done better with more education. The greatest factor in your favor is you jumped right in and tried. Rather than diminish your self-confidence, your failure should make you more determined than ever to try again and this time succeed. Remember, whether or not you succeed at everything you try is not important. What is important is the fact that you are the type of person who will succeed if you keep trying. Why? Because you have the courage to try. You are the type of person who will say to yourself, "Sometimes they'll see me win, sometimes they'll see me lose, but they'll never see me quit!"

What you perceived as failure was not really failure. You just made a mistake. Ask yourself the following questions to find out where you made that mistake. Did I chose the wrong type of product? Did I take time to think my plans through carefully enough before implementing them? Did I spend enough time and work hard? Was my timing wrong for this type of business?

Mistakes are only temporary. Learning from them is the important thing. The learning will build your self-confidence and in return help you become the successful person you want to be.

On this road to success, each day must be a day of achievement. The importance of consistently working to achieve your goals and encouraging yourself in your business should not be underestimated. Be smart enough to use your capabilities to succeed. Be determined to work hard enough to make your efforts succeed. Be strong enough to bounce back when you lose one round, and win the next one. Let each experience educate you and make you more determined to be the winner in the end. Have confidence in yourself to do whatever is necessary to succeed.

Keep right on all the time. Just remember, being successful is seldom easy. The only easy thing in success is the fun. Many times even the fun part disappears. But there are times when you will sit back, especially after you have accomplished a goal, and you'll think, "I never thought I'd get this far. I didn't think I'd ever get over that hurdle." But once you are over it, you will stick out your chest and think, "Wow, I did it! I can tackle anything now!" And believe me, something else will come up. There always seems to be a monkey wrench thrown into the gears to slow you down or stop you. Just determine within yourself that you will not be stopped.

Remember, this is a game, and you are going to win it. You can never win once you quit. No one has ever been smart enough or lucky enough to win every round. Be prepared to lose a few, but do not lose the game. Once you quit, you have lost all and your game of success is over.

7

GETTING YOURSELF TOGETHER

Many people do not start their own business because they are too busy trying to make a living. For some, there just aren't enough hours in a day to plan their ventures correctly and still work. Then there are others who are too busy watching television, sitting in bars sipping on beer, being lazy and doing nothing all day but complain about how bad life is to put any plans together to start a business. Many are so busy feeling sorry for themselves they can't see the potential hidden within them.

When you decide what you want to do, finding financial help or the right location involves many hours. Then, more time is needed to get the equipment and do the necessary planning. Where does one find all this time?

You must learn how to regulate your time. Every day make a list of your priorities. Once your list is completed, scan it and select the one that is most important, that must be done first. Then choose the second, third, and so forth. You now have your priorities in mind. Because you probably won't think of everything at one time, utilize your free time to add to your list as necessities occur to you. Keep it with you. Each time you complete a task or goal, cross it off. If your priorities change during the day, this will not affect your direction as long as you have taken care of the main priorities first. As your business grows from day to day, so will your list. The important thing is the organization of your time, not the length of your list. Your aim is to get into the habit of doing first things first.

Your list should be detailed, including even small, non-business responsibilities which need your attention, such as buying a birthday card, sending a bouquet of flowers to a friend, or calling your mother.

As you learn to list and carry through on the non-business and business areas of your life, the natural tendency to procrastinate will no longer exist.

I often make my list at home in the evening and put it with my keys to grab quickly as I leave for the office in the morning. By using the ideas I write down, I can plan my day more easily. Giving your day direction will help you become a more organized person. People who make their priority list from day to day, week to week, even month to month have a tendency to be more successful. Being organized is just as important for someone starting out in business as it is for that person who is already on their way to success with important business meetings to attend, investments to look after and a business to run. Saving time is important because time is money.

For your yearly planning, I suggest using your calendar. At the end of each year, determine goals you want to reach, and give those goals a date. Be specific with yourself. You will find your time will be better organized, and more necessary tasks will be completed when you let the unnecessary projects wait until you have spare time. Let me remind you, if you are going to run a business well, you will have very little spare time. You must learn to use all your time wisely.

While we are talking about regulating your time for your business, let's talk about the family. Your family, if you are a family person, plays an essential role in your plan. Your mate has to know about your plans and agree to go along with them. It will need to be understood that starting a business involves many long hours away from home. If your mate wants you home after an eight-hour day, you are in trouble. You cannot become as successful by working an eight-hour-a-day job. There may often be changes in meal time. While you will be sacrificing by spending long hours at work, your mate may be sacrificing by spending long hours at home alone. Theirs may actually be the greater sacrifice. Why? Because you are going into something you enjoy. Your mate will not enjoy your spending more time at work.

Is your mate willing to wait and sacrifice for success? What type of person is he or she? The sort who will go along with your desires and dreams and the need to work long hard hours? Or will they, as soon as you are achieving success, want a new home, new car, vacations and fancy clothes? Will they be willing to settle back and wait until the time is right for the rewards? Some people are willing to do this themselves, but their mates are not. Soon they find themselves in trouble, and out goes the marriage. If you start paying alimony, it is pretty hard to become rich. Right?

Don't hide what is involved. Work out these problems before you start your business. Be sure your mate understands, shares and is willing to go along with your dream. The more you can involve your mate in your plans and business, the more fun it becomes for both of you. When they have an understanding of what you are trying to accomplish, you then have a healthy arrangement.

Maybe you have children. What about them? You should enjoy and love them. You cannot enjoy them and share your love with them if you don't see them. That is one of the disadvantages of being successful, or trying to be successful. It is very hard, almost impossible, to run your business and also be at home. You cannot be with your family all the time. Most of your time will be spent on your business.

Consider how you can best use your time before or after business hours. You will have to determine for yourself how your time will be divided, and work that out in your daily schedule. Both areas of your life are important. I want you to succeed in your business as well as enjoy your family. You must give adequate time to both so you have no regrets. You cannot afford to neglect either one. Do not go through life so busily that one day you look at your children, realize they are already grown, and regret you didn't take time to enjoy them.

If they are playing in a music concert, be there. If they are going to a ball game, go with them. If they want to sit down and talk with you, you better be there and you better <u>listen.</u> I emphasize the word listen, because being there in body, but not giving your undivided attention, is not enough. It will not only cause hard feelings between you and your children, but you will miss out. Without the love and enjoyment of your children, your money will mean nothing. What good would it be to have success and money, but be a failure to your family? There is nothing more rewarding than sitting back and remembering the good times of playing, talking, or just plain enjoying your children.

Involve your children in your business by explaining various facets of your work to them. It develops their creativity while helping them understand why you are not home as much as they would like.

Talking things over with your mate and children can often give you a better understanding of your business, and may enable you to come up with ideas which otherwise might not have been considered. It will definitely help them understand you. It may even help you understand yourself better.

You may feel as I did about sharing the business with my family. I didn't spend much time talking about it. I tried to convince myself they were not interested, but they would have been interested if I had involved them more, or at least talked to them about it. No matter how much you want to, you can't completely separate your home and your business.

Being in business always involves problems. You may not want to burden your family with the problems or bring problems home. And yet, you may be able to work out many solutions after your children go to bed. In fact, after you go to bed. You may often lie awake for hours trying to solve problems that confront you. Those quiet hours can help you unravel many of them and generate new ideas. You then will have more time during the day to tend to your business.

Starting your business does involve all your family. They should be taken into consideration and consulted. However, you are the one who must make the final decision to take the ball and run with it. You must find the time to do what is necessary. The longer you put it off, the harder it will be to accumulate your wealth. Accumulating enough wealth to start investing takes a long time. The earlier in life you start, the better chance you have of becoming more successful. It will take many dedicated hours, even years, to accumulate your money and have your business grow to its fullest.

8

LEARNING HOW TO DO IT

A human being is special. He can learn what he needs to learn. The bear has his claws, the wolf has his nose, the hawk has his wings, but a man has his brain. If he uses his brain, he can survive. In this book we are contemplating not only survival, but also success and contentment.

You can learn how to run a business, even though the idea frightens you and the possibility of making it work profitably seems far past your imagination or ability. Nearly everyone feels that way in the beginning.

Two personal qualities are needed: gumption and self-confidence. Gumption is courage and initiative; enterprise and boldness. Self-confidence is simply belief in yourself. With these two internal characteristics working for you, you can figure out how to make your business work. As you begin to incorporate these qualities into your everyday life, you will gain strength.

I would like to share my experience in the grocery business with you as an illustration. I was young then, with abundant energy, but discontent in my present position. I realized I was not getting ahead fast enough. I needed something else, something I could make successful.

I found a small grocery store for sale and invested all my available funds, which wasn't very much. The size of the store did not hamper my dream one bit. I just made up my mind I was going to make it work and have my business grow with me. As you read this illustration, keep in mind that I knew very little about the grocery business.

Right from the start I said to myself, "I may not know how to run this store, but I am going to learn. I don't care if it takes me from five o'clock in the morning until two o'clock the next morning." In the beginning it almost did.

There were so many things I didn't know. I had to learn how to order and check in deliveries, cut produce to make it look good, cut meat, operate the machines, make attractive displays, advertise, and keep the books. But I learned. I had nothing but time.

The other markets in town were run by managers who, because their interests were not in the store, were usually "out for coffee". This observation resulted in an obvious conclusion for success on my part. I made up my mind I was going to be visible to my customers. That became a big plus for me. I also made sure I had better sales than they did.

My grocery store was in a small community, and most of my customers were farmers. When they came, I was busy, but conspicuous and available. I greeted all my customers by name, which made them feel as though they were coming to visit with an old friend when they walked into the store. I worked the cash register as often as possible and even carried out groceries, especially for those who came to shop alone. If a customer brought merchandise back that was unsatisfactory, or at least they thought so, I was just as happy to see them then as when they purchased it.

Do you know what happened? They loved my services! They loved it when I said hello to them, calling them by name. They loved it when I was up at the cash register, checking out and carrying out their groceries. Soon they weren't even looking at my sales anymore. They were coming to shop there because they felt comfortable and welcome. They were loving and enjoying the personal attention which is so valuable to all of us.

After a few years, my success was beginning to show and grow. And grow we did! I had approximately eighty percent of all the business in the area, even though my prices were sometimes higher. Expansion soon became necessary. An adjacent retail area was utilized, new produce and meat cases were purchased, and new tiling was laid on the floor. My establishment was always neat and clean and looked successful.

Once my success was apparent, the business became an object of desire for other businesses. Grocery chain outfits called me constantly, wanting to buy my grocery store, offering me many times more than the original purchase price. In just a short time, I had my store, my home, and my cars all paid for, plus money in the bank.

How did all this happen? I was willing to start small and grow in knowledge and success with my business. As my success grew, I never permitted myself to feel I was overly important. In addition to that, I had kept myself so busy I hadn't had time to spend the money I was accumulating. But mainly I succeeded because I did not forget the people who made me successful. I still said hello to them and called them by name. I still carried out their groceries. And I still did my share of the work. The bookkeeping had become easier, as well as the ordering, advertising, and displaying of meat and produce because I had taken time to learn my business just as I had determined to do, and I had learned it well. The personal services I had given my customers had paid off in great dividends and had cost me nothing.

This is an example of succeeding in a field you know nothing about but feel you can learn. I have told it mainly to give you direction and encouragement. If you want to succeed, and are willing to learn, you can do it. And you don't have to go into the grocery business. It could be hardware, or bicycles, or literally any of thousands of other available ventures. To succeed, you use the same tactics.

Let me state those tactics in compact form:

1. WATCH your competitors and find out where you can do better. Maybe it is in sales, or displays, or customer relations.

2. SHOW your customers that you and your help care about them as individuals and appreciate their business. Also, show your customers that you care about your business by being there when you are needed.

3. NEVER let yourself feel you are more important than you really are.

4. KEEP yourself so busy you don't have time to spend the money you are accumulating.

I want you to read tactic number four one more time. It is very important to your success. It states you should not take time to spend your income. The time you would use spending that hard-earned money should become time spent figuring out how to improve your business and building it by your work, plus studying and preparing yourself to buy investments. Once you are prepared and educated and have your plans working the way you want them to, your involvement becomes a game, a fun-game of success and riches full of personal rewards. Until then, depriving yourself of immediate pleasures is essential to success.

Life is a series of learning processes. You and your business progress the same way. You must learn to make your way step by step. Your experiences right now are as important as what you are anticipating when your plans are fulfilled and you find yourself a winner.

9

FINANCING YOUR BUSINESS

One of the priorities at the top of your list will be obtaining finances to open and maintain your business. The lack of ready available capital should not be a hinderance to you. There are many businesses which require little capital to start. In most instances, I do not want you to pay interest on financing, but there are times when you need to do so in order to establish your credit. The best place to go for your main source of financing is your local bank where you do business. Talk to your banker. He can explain various types of government guaranteed financing available for starting a business and suggest the best one to suit your needs. This is the beginning of your excellent credit rating. Keep your payments current. It is almost impossible to start or run a business without some sort of credit.

Hopefully you have a good credit rating. If you do not, you will have more difficulty proving to your loan officer you are capable of borrowing money and paying it back. Your past credit history is a strong, valuable argument for you and your banker in determining if you should get a loan.

Establishing credit takes a lot of planning and should not be taken lightly. The earlier you start establishing credit the better. Be certain to pay close attention to it. Make it a top priority to keep it good. No matter how long you are in business or how old you are, you will usually want some form of credit. Credit planning sessions with your banker will help you establish your credit and keep it good. When starting out, it can help you get your business off the ground. Then the money you earn from your business will, in turn, make more credit available to you. Even if you don't use it, it is convenient to have at your finger tips.

Although banks are in the business of lending money, they want to lend money to people who will pay them back. If your credit is good, that should be of some encouragement to you. But your good credit alone will not convince them you know what you are doing, or that your business will pay off for you and for them. The first step in getting financing is to have a good plan thoroughly thought out and legibly written, preferably typed. All credit references should be documented. This information is essential to your banker. Once your documentation is ready, go to your loan officer, and present your plan. This information will prove to him that you have thought out your plan and you will succeed.

If you are starting a retail business, your documentation should:

1. Show how much inventory you will need. (The amount of sales which you project will determine how much inventory you need.) This will determine how much you will need to borrow.

2. Determine what your profit will be. Project your income for the year from the sale of your merchandise, less the cost.

3. List all other expenses. Some of these will include rent, utilities, insurance, salaries, taxes and living expenses. If you still have a good return after subtracting all your expenses plus your loan payment and living expense from your projected gross, then you should be able to convince your banker.

If you are starting a professional or service-oriented business, follow the same rules:

1. Determine how much it will cost to set up your business, including furniture, tools or machinery and supplies.

2. Estimate what your services will bring in per

year. (Some months may be slower than others so you need to use an average.)

3. Determine all your expenses for the year including your loan payment. Deduct this from your projected income.

4. The result will be your Net Income. This will be the determining factor for you and your banker whether your business will succeed or fail.

Whenever you start any business, you have to estimate your income and expenses. It is very important to spend much time determining them. Be certain not to estimate your income too high or figure your expenses too low. Where and how you obtain this information is important also. Your documentation should include how you determined your expenses and your projected sales/income. This information is not only for your banker. It is for your use also. If you cannot prove this venture will succeed and be profitable, why even attempt it? It would be better to try a venture that will succeed.

When you meet with your loan officer, dress neatly, in a business-like manner. You must look and act like a successful business person. Be confident in yourself and your business. If you are married, you may want to take your mate along with you. This gives your loan officer the chance to meet and judge both of you. Never be afraid to look him in the eye and let him know you mean business. If you have a good plan and your credit is good, you should have very little trouble getting a loan. Your main objective is to convince your bank you are going to succeed.

If you have tried every means possible to convince your bank you are going to succeed, and they still turn you down, your next step would be to borrow the money from a relative, a close friend, or a business associate. This route should only be taken if it is absolutely necessary.

If you are borrowing from a friend or relative, the same rules apply as when borrowing from a bank. That is, you should have a well thought-out, documented plan. Your agreement to pay them back should be in writing, and all terms should be clearly understood and explained. It should definitely be a business transaction and not taken lightly. There are some people who feel if a friend or relative lends them money, they do not have to pay them back. This is totally false. If you have a friend or relative willing to lend you money to start your business, you must be just as willing to pay them back, as though they were a bank.

Sometimes friends and relatives want a percentage of your business, and they usually want their money back quickly. I recommend paying them interest rather than offering them a percentage. In fact, you should pay them interest. You may even have to pay them a little more interest than the bank would require of you. Keep in mind that your payment and interest can only be so high. Sit down and figure out what you feel you can afford to pay and be in control of the situation, or you may get yourself and the lender in trouble.

There are times when you may need to take a partner on to obtain your financing. Before you take this step, determine whether both of your families can make enough to live on and still run your business successfully. A partnership may not be feasible if splitting the income takes too much out of the business. That has to be taken into consideration before you commit yourself. Any partnership should not be taken lightly and should be avoided if possible. This form of financing should be a last resort.

If you commit yourself to a partnership, make certain everything is documented. It is very crucial that everything in your agreement is written, understood, and accepted by all parties. The agreement should be legally signed and witnessed by an uninvolved party. All involved parties should have their own copy of the agreement.

If your partner is a relative or friend, you may think a handshake, or a smile, or just a nonchalant conversation across a table while having a cup of coffee or lunch should settle the deal. Definitely not! It is important for you to treat this agreement as strictly business. Follow the guidelines I have listed above to eliminate trouble in later years. Your trouble, if it starts, may be five or ten years from now. If you do not have everything written down and understood, there could be problems and hard feelings. Friendships often disintegrate over money.

Once you get your financing, pay special attention to it. Keeping good credit will take careful planning and sound judgment on your part. A good credit rating is absolutely essential to any business person, no matter what size your business is. I urge you to make all payments a few days in advance, and never later than agreed. When your payments are due, you must have adequate money with which to pay them.

If for some reason you do have a problem making a payment or two, never wait for the bank to contact you. It is imperative for you to contact them first, in person, not by telephone. Go to the creditor and explain why you cannot make your payment(s). Set up a payment plan you can meet. Then by all means, follow through on the plan.

You must be as anxious to pay your loan payments on time as you were to get the loan the day you applied for it. Without a bank behind you, you will have difficulty succeeding in your business. No matter what size your business is, a good relationship with your bank is essential. You will need it when you want to expand or need extra working capital. As you grow in business, you will grow with your bank. Your relationship should be very close and friendly.

Probably the most convenient credit source you can estab-lish with your bank is a type of loan called "Line of Credit." This may be unfamiliar to some of you. There is no set limit that I know of on this type of loan and it can be useful in many ways. It depends only on your ability to pay and the strength of your credit rating. You and your banker will determine what your business will require.

Once your Line of Credit is approved, you can call your banker and request the amount you need in your checking account, up to the limit of your loan. Because your credit is pre-approved and estab-lished, the finances are immediately available to you, as long as you stay within your loan limit. Another advantage is you do not have to pay interest on that money until you withdraw it. Your loan will have to be renewed each year, and most banks require you to have a zero balance for at least one month of the year. The details concerning your individual Line of Credit will have to be discussed with your banker.

10

HANDLING YOUR CASH FLOW

While financing is of primary importance, it is not the only consideration. On the road to success you have to learn to think ahead. You must have a good financial plan. Without it you will not succeed.

Financial strategy, the way you handle and disburse your money while you are making it, can be a determining factor in your winning the game. You must realize that all the income you have is not spendable. Your total income is your Gross Income. Your Net (or spendable) Income is what is left over after all your bills and obligations are met.

Let's dwell on that a bit. Say, for instance, you have an income of $10,000 for the month. That $10,000 goes into your checking account, and out of it you pay rent, utilities, car expenses, materials and supplies, insurance, loan payments, salaries, withholdings, interest, taxes, etc. You may have inventory to replace. Your income tax will be due quarterly, or at the end of the year. These quarterly or yearly expenses must be figured into your monthly budget. Your budget may consume more than two-thirds of your income. Not included in the budget are those miscellaneous expenses which occur without warning. All these have to come out of your $10,000. How carefully you control your expenses will determine your net income. The amount left over, your Net Spendable, is your real income. How that real income is utilized will determine your success.

Expenses are ever-present. Be aware of when those expenses are due. Go over them at least once a month. Know what they are, and determine where you can cut down on them in the future. Never spend more than you can afford. Never assume that the balance remaining in your checkbook at the end of the month is yours to spend. You may get caught in your own trap by spending money which is not rightfully yours, but will be due for other expenses. Constantly remind yourself that all your income is not spendable. Remember, it doesn't matter how much money you make. If you spend it all, you still end up with nothing!

You will notice that once you manage to get one credit card, every credit card company in the business is anxious to give you one. They know where their money is...in the compulsive buyer. They make money on your outstanding balance because you have to pay a high rate of interest on it. To buy now and pay later is a temptation which is not readily resisted in our society. It is so easy to accumulate "things", racking up debts which we have to pay later.

For example, consider the person who ended up with numerous credit cards and, due to compulsive buying, soon found they were thousands of dollars in debt. Or consider the couple whose income dropped from $100,000 to $30,000 a year. Unfortunately, their spending and lifestyle was geared to the higher income and, because they were unwilling to give it up, they were soon deeply in debt.

According to the International Credit Association, an estimated twenty-four million consumers have trouble paying their bills. Generally, consumers hold and use too many credit cards. They have a tendency to live on their gross income, rather than on their real income. The problem stems from making credit an easy option and putting a priority on material goods. In our age of plenty, people never seem to prepare themselves for a financial crunch. The four factors combined which generally do most people in are: living on one income, unrealistic budgeting, unforeseen expenses, and a reluctance to face the truth about expenses.

If you fit into any of those categories, and especially the last one, the following suggestions should be helpful to you:

1. If you are paying only the minimum payment on your credit card bills, you are getting nowhere. Get out your calculator now and find out how deeply in debt you really are.

2. Decide if you can handle the problem your-

self or do you need professional help. Do not consider bankruptcy unless it is your final resort. Bankruptcy remains on your credit for ten years. Consider first consolidating your debts into one payment. If you need help, contact a local credit counselor or your banker.

3. Your biggest step in resolving your debt situation is to stop using your credit cards. If you don't want to cut them in half, lock them up. If you have the willpower, I suggest keeping one handy in case of an emergency, and promise yourself that you will pay it off each month.

4. Then start saving, as I mentioned earlier. Squeeze whatever you can out of your new budget, whether it is $5 or $50 a week. Remember, a small nest egg is better than a pocket full of plastic.

The impulse to spend all your income is not surprising. If you are new to the world of business-ownership, you are probably used to living on a fixed income. People that have had regular jobs with a set income each month are used to spending that income and budgeting themselves accordingly. Generally, saving is not habitual. If that description fits you, when unexpected expenses arrive, you may find yourself unprepared mentally, as well as financially. Begin training yourself to expect the unexpected.

How you handle your money affects all areas of your life. Some people make large sums of money, but never advance financially, because they have never taken time to learn how to control their money. You must be determined to make money, but you must also be determined to handle that money wisely. Some of the income will be needed to live on, but most of it should be reinvested in your business. If you do not reinvest your earnings, you will probably see your business fail, rather than see it grow. If that happens, you will have wasted an opportunity for financial success and enriched self-esteem. So, use your money for operation and growth, and later on for investments.

In your business, your first investment will probably be equipment and inventory. Investing in good, fast equipment will increase your productivity. If it saves you time, it will ultimately save you money. Be sure you are getting the best merchandise for the least amount of money. Even if you buy an established business, you should request information from suppliers other than those used by the previous owner.

If you cannot afford to pay cash for your inventory, you will have to finance it. Every time you finance something, you pay interest. To me, interest can be either beneficial or detrimental. If you are <u>receiving</u> the interest, it is beneficial; if you are <u>paying</u> interest, it is detrimental. Avoid paying interest as often as you can, but if paying interest in relationship to your business is profitable, it can be excusable. It is always a good idea to use your credit to make more profits. If you want to reach the top, your money must work for you. Credit used properly can bring you good profits.

To sum this up, if you can justify paying interest by acquiring more merchandise, buying income property, or making other investments, then paying interest is advisable because you are borrowing money to make more money. As long as you can prove that your investment is good enough to pay that interest and still show a profit, go ahead and invest. The interest you pay is tax deductible, as is the depreciation on your building and your equipment.

Your first investment, separate from your business, will probably be your home. This really should be the first time you are paying interest, except on your business. Purchasing a home is an investment. If you pay rent, you receive nothing back. If the home you are renting makes your family happy, it might be worthwhile to buy that home and pay interest. Even though you are going to live in it, if you purchase it correctly it will eventually make you money. A home, as with all real estate, is a hedge against inflation. It most likely will increase in value, but at the same time you will be deducting the interest from your income taxes, while the remainder of your payment will go toward the principal. Unlike other investments, it is an investment you can enjoy while paying for it. Although stock is an investment and may be paying off, you cannot really enjoy it unless you sell it and spend the money. You do not have to sell your home to enjoy its benefits.

But again, be cautious. Do not overextend yourself. Your main purpose, when starting out, is to build a solid base for the future and, as always, establish a good credit rating.

The question you need to ask yourself is whether you can handle the money you are about to make. Are you the type who is going to spend before you really should? Early in the game you must learn it is harder to control money than it is to make it. Many people make lots of money but never learn how to control it. Others lose money making poor investments. Don't spend your money before you make it, and don't waste it after you've made it.

Waiting for the right time to buy is very important. It is amazing how many people go shopping for something they need, and just because they are out looking, they feel they have to buy. When purchasing any major item, don't be in a hurry to buy, and always be certain you get the best price available. When you want to buy a personal item, ask yourself if you really need it. If you are getting along without it, why not wait? An effective safeguard to use, whenever you get the urge to buy, is to take that money and invest it. When your investment has made enough money to pay for the item, then reconsider buying it. Putting this theory into practice works wonders. Spending money on personal items will make that money unavailable to your business.

Many people have been on the brink of success, but because they spent their money, even to the point of going in debt and paying interest, they have fallen by the wayside. The surest road to failure is to buy items such as furniture, appliances, cars, and vacations on time, and pay interest on them. Don't let this happen to you. Every time you put your name on the dotted line agreeing to pay interest, you are going to have to work and spend valuable time to pay for that interest. You want to be earning interest, not paying it. Your time will come! Be patient! Do not let yourself get into the habit of thinking you must have something immediately, just because you want it. Patience is a lesson you must learn. If you really feel you need that item or vacation, wait until you can pay for it.

For instance, there are people who will go out and buy a new car without taking into consideration the full cost. Let's look at a typical example. Suppose you are about to purchase a new car for $10,000. You have $2,000 for a down payment. The amount you will need to finance is $8,000. On top of that will be a $50 loan fee, making your total loan $8,050. With your interest at the annual percentage rate of 10.93%, if you finance that car for a five year/60 payment term, your payments will be approximately $174 per month. In the end, you will pay the bank approximately $10,420 for the use of their $8,050, (that is over $2,400 in interest and loan charges), plus your $2,000 cash down which you could have invested.

You must also remember it is not just the interest you are paying. You also have to figure your down payment. For instance, let's look at the $2,000 you put down on the $10,000. If you had taken that $2,000 and put it in savings at 5% for five years, you would have made over five hundred dollars. By paying the down payment and then financing the remaining $8,000, you are actually losing the interest you could have gained on your savings, plus paying interest on the balance. The $2,000 you invested in your new car will cost you approximately $6,000 in five years. It will cost you approximately $3,900 in interest and insurance, plus you could have invested that money at 10% which would have yielded a profit of $2,048. Do you still want to buy that new car? Now you can see why paying interest will restrict your determination to become wealthy and successful.

My emphasis is, wait until you can afford it and pay cash!

If you start by financing a car, then finance your business, and later finance your home, your purchases will actually cost you money rather than let you make money. You will find yourself working to pay interest rather than to make money. You are not working to pay someone else interest and make them rich. You are working to make yourself rich. Interest is money you have to earn. Money earned takes valuable time. If you spend too much of your valuable time earning money to pay interest, your chances of being successful start deteriorating. It all reverts back to your planning and patience.

I know I am beginning to sound as if I do not want you to finance anything. That is not true. There are times when you have to finance. Your responsibility will be to plan how much you can afford in payments. When you consider financing some-thing and paying interest on it, will you come out ahead by doing so? If you can answer "Yes," then go ahead and finance.

You may be asking, "What fun is it being successful if I can't spend anything?" Sometimes the enjoyment comes from just making money, having it available, and knowing you can spend it when you want. Then saving and investing money becomes more fun than spending. The choice is yours. You will have to decide when you want to start spending and how much you want to spend. The more you spend, the less you will have to invest. The less you invest, the less income you will receive. The less income you receive from investments, the harder and longer you will have to work. If you spend too much, you will limit your success. It's as simple as that.

Some people don't have to be rich, they just want some extra money. That is fine too. Whatever is good for you. My goal in life was to have lots of security, to live in luxury, and to have plenty of income. I wanted my investments working and making money for me when I retired. Now, while I am away, my investments are still working for me and paying off. I know my income is still growing. That, to me, is real enjoyment. That is what I worked and planned for. That is what made it all worthwhile, and you can have this, too.

You are probably saying I make it sound easy. I am not trying to make it sound that way at all. It is not easy becoming wealthy. It is hard work. Many of you who read this book are not going to attain the gold we are working towards, because becoming rich takes work, planning, determination, and patience, and you are looking for the easy way out.

To the people who say, "Why make this money if I can't spend it?" I say, you can spend it later. You can spend money when you can't keep up with your investments. When the interest, rent payments, and stock dividends you are receiving start bringing in so much money you can't spend it all, then you can spend. You can have a ball taking your trips or fulfilling your wildest dreams, as long as when you return you have as much or more money than when you went away. When you do this, then you have achieved your Gold!

Most people do not stop working even after they start feeling rich. You probably won't either, because that is when the fun of success really begins.

Handling your money wisely is a long-range project which you will have to learn. It's not just how you spend your money today. You must plan your financial strategies for your future as well. Never neglect your regular financial responsibilities. Never be afraid to reinvest your earnings, whether it be in your business or other invest-ments. Investing is the name of success and can only bring profitable returns when invested correctly.

I am going to briefly restate these Five Keys to Success for you. (1) Have confidence in yourself and in what you are going to do, and then do it. (2) If you don't know how to manage your time, determine within yourself that you are going to learn. (3) When you have chosen your business, figure out how you are going to make that business work by using your own ideas. (4) Establish and maintain a good credit rating to assure availability of working capital. (5) Handle your finances properly.

Remember, we are going for the gold, not the bronze. There will be times when you will win, there will be times when you will lose, but we will never see you quit.

PART III

BEING #1

11

MAKING IT WORK

By now you are ready to start your venture (adventure). Two factors come immediately into play: Does your community really need your business and how well will you run it? If you have too much good, direct competition in the area in which you want to establish yourself, then it is possible that, no matter how hard or how well you run your business, you may not succeed. A business does not automatically succeed because you start it. It would be worth your while to establish yourself in an area that has less competition. If your business is poorly-run, it will not benefit your community or you. If you are going to attempt to establish a business, you should determine to do it right. Keep in mind, if you fail and quit, you not only fail in your business, but you also lose the chance to wear many other hats which could be yours as the result of succeeding.

TIMING

One question you must ask yourself: Is the timing right for this type of business?

Proper timing is essential. Sometimes you can recognize indicators in the economy. At other times, the government's control of the economy affects your business. Sometimes it is the combination of luck, local or national economy, and governmental influence which help you achieve your most effective performance, thus making your business profitable. You must continually do your homework, before and after you start your business.

If you want to open a retail business, the value and buying power of the consumer's dollar must always be considered when you are purchasing your inventory. On what commodities is the consumer spending his dollar? Research these facts, then decide how to promote your product or services to make the most attractive presentation to your prospective customers.

A few decades ago, when the "Tinker Man" came to the door, everything was put aside, and he was given quality-time to display his wares. The buyers knew it would be a long time before he came by again. Today, customers are very mobile. They are not dependent on you alone for the service they need. They can go next door to your competitor. Therefore, you must protect your investment by moving in time with the economy. Keep a close eye on government trends and determine their relationship to your business. If inflation is rising, interest rates will rise, and the consumer will tighten his belt. If you are selling luxury items and have an overextended inventory, you may be hurt or ruined.

When there are no real, recognizable indicators, timing becomes a factor you cannot control.

Recently, when interest rates were extremely high, real estate, car sales, and the market for major purchases were very depressed. The chances that someone new to business could have seen that trend coming would have been unlikely. For example, someone starting in car-sales just before the rise in interest rates would have failed to read the signs in time, and would have had too large an inventory on hand due to slow sales. High interest rates, combined with slow sales, newness of the business, and lack of cash reserve would probably cause that business to fail. The seasoned business person would have reduced his inventory when interest rates started to rise. But many older, more established companies also found themselves in trouble because they misjudged their timing and didn't see the economic trend.

In an instance such as this, if you have a cash reserve and manage to reduce your inventory in time, you may survive. If you do survive, people will say you "lucked out." That is actually a correct statement concerning the fortune of a good, successful business person. But remember, you make your own luck. If you are sharp enough, you will be lucky. If you aren't, you will be unlucky! I want you to notice I did not say smart enough, I said sharp enough. You do not

66

necessarily need to be smart to be sharp and successful.

NEED

Here is the second question you must ask yourself: Is your type of business needed?

Suppose you want to start a small grocery store. In your neighborhood there is a large chain grocery, a Seven-Eleven down the street, and a liquor store that handles food-stuffs. On the corners of a main intersection are two service stations handling most of the high-profit items you need to sell in order to make a success of your business. But, down the street is a vacant building with low rent. You already have your living quarters established, so this would be an easy way to get started. If you open up your store in that type of situation, I am quite sure you will have bad luck. That bad luck will probably be blamed on everything and everyone, except the one who created it, you.

Now let's turn that around. Let's say you are sharp enough to find a small town grocery where there is very little competition. The store is dirty, its shelves look messy, it never has any good sales, the meat counter looks as though it should be dumped into the garbage, and the few people who work in the store are too busy telling each other what they did last night to wait on you. When you look out the two big windows in the front of the store, you aren't sure if the sun is shining or not, because the windows haven't been washed for three years. This store needs help!

So, you round up the owner and make him an offer he cannot refuse (very little). If he is not smart enough to take that "very little" with a lot less down, and terms you can live with, find yourself a building as close to his as possible. Paint and clean it. Clean your windows until they sparkle. Buy some good (used, if necessary) equipment, and go to work. Get some nice fresh fruit and vegetables in your produce section and some good-looking meat in your meat counter. Stack your newly-built shelves neatly with good products at competitive prices. Hang some big signs on those sparkling windows advertising good sale items. Hire a couple of people who weren't out last night, and you're ready for business.

Then listen to your competition down the street complain to everyone about how you moved in and lucked out by stealing all his customers. If you do your "work" correctly, you can only succeed.

In the first situation, to start a business in an area already saturated would be unprofitable. You would be fighting too much competition. The location of your building "down the street" might be away from the direct flow of traffic, which is another factor against you. If there are too many factors against your success, you need to look at another type of business or a different area.

The second situation is ideal. No one likes to shop in a dirty store. Sparkling windows, good sales, and friendly service will bring customers flocking to your doorstep. Everyone likes to receive attention when they enter a place of business, and an attentive sales force is good for business.

So, find yourself a business you are capable of running, in an area that is in need of such a business, and fulfill that need. Remember, if you don't know how to do it, you can always learn. Experience, by trial and error, is a great teacher.

Do you live in a neighborhood where people own animals which need grooming, but where the nearest place of service is twenty miles away? Do you like animals? Learn to groom them, and open your own business.

Are you good with plants and landscaping? Do you like the outdoors? Does your neighborhood have large homes with huge yards and double-income families who don't have the time for upkeep? Start a landscaping business.

Do you like children? Are there working parents or single parents in your neighborhood who need day care services? Open a day care center.

Are you handy with wood? Can you repair furniture? Open an upholstery or cabinet-making business.

Do you enjoy sports activities but the only sport shop in town is outdated? Open your own. Stock up with the latest sports equipment. Consider the advantages of dealing with sales and rentals. Get involved in all sports programs.

Do you enjoy repairing appliances? Do you love antiques? Are you interested in electronics?

These are only a few of the millions of opportunities available to the person who is willing to work. There are many fields you can go into which you presently know nothing about, but are capable of learning. In many cases, it would be better to buy an existing business. If the only business in town is failing, or the owner wants to retire because of illness or a death in the family, make the owner an offer.

FRANCHISE

If you want to buy a business, should you consider franchising?

The first franchised business began in the early 1700's in Great Britain when an industrious ale producer distributed his ale to various pubs. Then came Singer, who used the same idea to boost sewing machine sales. After World War II, franchising became popular. Among the early pioneers were A&W Root Beer, Baskin and Robbins, and Hertz Rent-a-Car. The International Franchising Association predicts that by the year 2010, one-half of all retail dollars will be generated by franchise.

What is franchising? A franchise is simply a method of distributing products and services. A franchisee pays an initial fee to a franchisor who has offered his or her trademark, trade name, and business system, which grants the right to use them. Some of the benefits of buying into a reputable franchise are:

1. Proven methods of operation
2. Guidance in finding the right location
3. Proven building plans, if necessary
4. Financing usually available
5. Benefits of national advertising
6. Advertisement assistance locally
7. Availability of necessary equipment
8. Use of name and products
9. Pre-organized bookkeeping system

The franchisor receives royalties on the income accumulated. A typical home-based franchise usually costs less, sometimes as little as $2,000. The risk involved is lower and profits earned are potentially greater because you have less overhead and simpler payroll, tax, maintenance, and insurance requirements.

If you are considering buying a franchise, there are some questions you need to have answered before you sign on the dotted line. The Uniform Franchise Offering Circular will be of great help to you in this area. It should provide you with a financial disclosure and background information of the business in which you are interested as well as a list of franchisees' addresses and phone numbers. Contact your local library for current information regarding this publication.

Before making your decision, check out more than one franchise in your area of interest. Also contact as many franchisees as possible. Check the company's reputation and credit rating. Consult a franchise lawyer, accountant and your business advisor before signing the franchise agreement and any other contracts you are asked to sign. Set up a tax plan, make financial projections for one to five years, and determine the sales potential in your area before you commit yourself.

Naturally there are questions you must ask yourself concerning your decision. Here are a few pertinent ones:

1. With my background, can I succeed in this field? This reverts back to Knowing Yourself. Consider your interests and skills when making a decision.

2. Can I financially afford to operate this business until it turns a profit?

3. Am I genuinely enthused about the business or do I just want to start one? Success comes easier when you are enjoying what you are doing.

4. Do I feel the franchise fees are too high?

5. Will the royalties balance out with potential profits and sales?

6. Am I being pressured into a decision?

7. Does the service meet a local demand? Is there

a lot of competition in this area?

8. Am I good at following rules and instructions? Independent thinkers may have a problem functioning within the confines of the franchise.

9. Is this firm interested in a long-term relationship or will their interest end once they get their fee?

10. Is the franchisor going to check my background and abilities? A good franchisor will.

11. Do I have to purchase all my supplies through the company? If so, are the prices competitive?

12. Are there other franchisees in my territory? If so, can both succeed?

13. Can I sell, trade or convert my franchise?

14. What are the renewal terms?

15. Am I or is the company responsible for warranties and   guarantees?

One more word of caution concerning buying a franchise. If you are dealing with a franchise broker or responding to an advertisement, insist on speaking to a company representative or employee before you sign any papers or pay any money.

Once you have narrowed the field down to a particular franchise, these are some questions you will need to ask the franchisor himself or herself:

1. How long has the franchisor been in business?
2. How well do the executives know their company?
3. How long has the firm offered franchises?

4. How many are in the operation?

5. Is a financial statement of the company available?

LOCATION

If you decide to start your own business rather than buy someone out or transact for a franchise, you must ask yourself, "What location would be best for me?"

There is a perfect location for the type of business you want to start. You will have to work as hard finding the right location as you will have to work once you open your business. I suggest contacting a local bank or the Chamber of Commerce in the area you want to locate your business, and ask them for advice.

Remember the old saying about location, location, LOCATION? I firmly believe in that! The location you choose should not be taken lightly. If you save money on one location, but lose business because of it or have to spend more on advertising, that is not the location you need. A few dollars more a month will mean nothing if you have the right location for your type of business, and it may mean the difference between success and failure.

Some types of businesses do not need a good location. A repair service needs an area easily accessible by car. A window washing business needs only a telephone. If you have a service-type business, you would be foolish to spend extra money just to watch the traffic go by. If you don't need traffic, don't pay for it. Get yourself an office or place of business outside the high-rent district or operate from your home.

On the other hand, if you start a ladies' apparel business, you need a location with lots of foot traffic and close to other similar businesses, such as downtown, on a busy street, or in a shopping mall. Naturally, this will put you in the expensive rent area, but to start it somewhere else would be self-defeating.

For instance, what if you want to start a bicycle shop? If you have the choice of putting it next to an old folks home or a college, why not put it next to the college and get lucky?

SELLING YOURSELF

Now that you have found the perfect location for your business, have prepared it, and are ready to go to work, you may be asking the question, "How do I promote my business and sell myself?" In other words, where and how do I get my customers?

When you own and run your own business, your biggest challenge is selling your product or service. Many professionals who provide great services become speechless when it comes to selling themselves. They love their work but feel awkward "selling themselves". Selling yourself should become an integral part of selling your product and service. Here are some ideas which will help you in your selling and make your negotiations professional.

1. Believe in your business and service. Think service rather than sales. Selling is like a conversation and the exploration of someone's thoughts, feeling and needs. Each contact should be approached with the "How can I help?" attitude, rather than "How much can I sell?" Promising good, long-term service goes a long way, especially if you keep your word.

2. Begin your sales efforts with people or businesses you think could use your services. Think of some area in which to benefit their business. For instance, you have a window-washing business and you notice a particular store could use some help with their windows. Maybe that same business has a lovely floral display in front of the building to accent it, but the windows are so dirty it detracts from the beauty of the arrangement. Contact the business, mention these two facts, and offer your services.

Making a warm call (one where you already know the need) is easier than making a cold call to a faceless name or an unknown business.

3. Rather than asking your customer to buy, ask if they are interested. If you get a no, ask why not. If the

prospect has a good reason, agree with them. Then proceed with additional information about your product or service to alleviate their concerns.

4. You never know who your next client will be, so treat everyone you meet as a prospect. Selling is the building of relationships. Most relationships are built on questions asked and answered by the parties involved. If you feel you have a hard time developing conversations with new clients, pretend you are interviewing them on the radio. You can ask such questions as: How long have you been in business? How did it get started? Do you like it? Is it growing? What do you see for your business in the years ahead? Then as you listen closely to what your prospect is telling you, you can adapt your approach to his or her needs. They will be more willing to listen to you because you were interested enough to ask about them. People also like to talk about their families or hobbies. This is an excellent way to get them to open up to you.

Once you have a customer interested enough to listen, you are ready to negotiate. There is a knack to negotiating professionally. Some business people are born negotiators who view negotiating as a game and excel in the art of making a deal. But others find it a frightening experience. Here are a few tips which should help:

1. Go into your negotiations with a plan. Doing so will boost your self-confidence and increase the likelihood of your success.

2. Define exactly what you want.

3. Set yourself three points to negotiate from, ranging from the highest possible position attainable, to your real goal, to your walk-away point.

4. Don't short-sell yourself or let yourself be

pressured into an unacceptable deal. If your deal is not what you want, walk away from it. Determining your negotiating position in advance gives you the liberty to concentrate on what is being said during the negotiations, rather than planning your responses.

Remember, if you can't sell what you do, you won't be doing it for very long.

THE WORK PLACE

Your approach to your customers will be influenced by the kind of office you keep, whether you have a retail or service-type business. You may be asking, "What do I need as furnishings?"

Need is the key word here. Decide what you need, not what you want. Your office is for you to function in efficiently, but it does not have to be a showplace. Don't be afraid to start small. Let yourself get the feel of your business. Don't go into debt to buy furniture; use that money for inventory or investments! Having a fancy office is not necessary in most cases. As time goes by and your success grows, you can feel justified in having your beautiful office. You will have earned it. But let's wait.

If you have a business where your clientele call on you, your office should be inviting and look successful. A home office-equipment system, including a computer, printer, multi-line phone, and the right software will give you the tools to run your business. But it won't be your furniture that will impress them. It will be the quality of your work and services. Use your creative ability to give your office the personality you want it to have. It is important to look successful. People are impressed when they walk into a nicely decorated office, but that can be accomplished without spending large sums of money.

Whether your customers come to you or you go to them, keeping your office neat and tidy will help you service them fast and efficiently. You need to be able to locate information when you need it. Neatness should extend into the remainder of your business or work area. Right here I want to make an important point. It seems as if our forefathers were better at keeping their work areas in order than the present generation. They seemed to have more pride in their projects. My point is, take pride in your work, whatever you do. If you have a business with large grounds, such as contractors or construction equipment businesses, keep those grounds neatly maintained. If you have a store or sales lot, keep supplies and materials neat and orderly. Know what you have and where it is.

Be very careful when ordering inventory. Ordering inventory is difficult if you don't have your stock properly arranged. This applies to anyone, but the person who is new to business must be especially cautious. Inventory that doesn't move takes up room in the warehouse and in the store, and uses capital that could be used to order good, saleable merchandise. If you have extremely slow-moving merchandise, put it on sale or dispose of it in some other manner, so you can use your space for saleable merchandise.

HIRING

Another question the new entrepreneur asks is "When do I start hiring employees?"

The more hiring you do, the less chance you have of succeeding. Your first responsibility to your business is to know it thoroughly. Hiring employees too soon will prevent you from gaining the knowledge you will need to help you deal with employee situations. You, as an employer, must first have carried the weight before you can give your employees an incentive to work well. Never ask your help to do something you have not done, or would not do yourself. As your business grows and you hire employees, your help will respect you more knowing you have done the actual work in your business.

Your most important goal in starting a business is to make money. The secret to making money is working so hard for so many hours you don't have time to spend what you are making, as I have stated so many times before. My answer to the question above is to delay hiring personnel as long as possible, and keep yourself busy. When you feel that your customer is not getting service of the best quality, and your business is starting to suffer because of it, that is the time to hire.

Don't expand your business so fast you can't control it. If it grows too fast, you may not have time to train your help correctly. Your business may suffer, and you may lose the business you now have. Don't get overanxious. Many people have failed in business because they expanded too soon. Not having enough trained help is a very common cause of failure.

Before hiring anyone, always keep in mind it isn't just the hiring of a person that is involved. Having employees is expensive. You must have a great enough need for their services to justify hiring them. After hiring, you have to train them. Their salary, social security, and withholdings have to be paid. If you feel the employees will not pay for themselves, then don't hire them.

When you decide you definitely need some help, consider carefully the type of person you will hire. Hire someone who will be an asset to your type of business, who will represent you fairly, and who has your business interest at heart. At times, you will have to hire someone who knows more about one part of the business than you do. There is nothing wrong with that. Hiring good, qualified people is the best way to complement your business. But hiring a better qualified person does not mean you are excused from understanding that position. On the contrary! You must remain in control.

It is important to find out if the prospective employee has the creative abilities needed to be an asset to your business. The more employees you hire whose abilities and interests coincide with your business, the more benefit you will receive. They will be happier on the job, and teaching them the business will be easier because they are working at what interests them. Being selective in your hiring will not only help you achieve your goals, but will also help your employees on their road to success by teaching them to use their gifted abilities.

Check your applicants carefully. Every employee, from busboy to top management, should be especially chosen and qualified for their position. Take time to observe and listen carefully. Study their applications or resumes before meeting them. Check their references. Watch for signs of excessive drinking or smoking, which might interfere with their productivity. Look for friendliness and cooperation in their conversation. Be sure your personalities will not clash and that they will be able to work with other employees.

Some types of questions are basic to a good interview.

Why do you want to work at this type of business?
What qualifications and training do you have?
How much experience do you have in this line of work?
Why are you looking for another position?
What creative abilities do you have?
What are your hobbies?
What are your likes and dislikes?
What are some things you would not like to do in this job?
What are your dreams and ambitions?

Naturally, you are going to have specific questions relating to your type of business. These are offered only as suggestions to give you direction in analyzing your prospective employees.

TRAINING

When training employees, your focus of attention will be on this question: Do your employees realize their responsibility is to give quality service to your customers?

So many times employers take it for granted that hired people know what is expected of them. The more time you spend with your employees, letting them know what will be expected of them and teaching them, the more productive they will be. And of course, that is what makes good business.

Good training in customer service starts at the top. During your employee's training period, make sure you are there to set the example. New employees should be trained to greet, treat, and service your customers. They must understand that when a customer is in need of help, the employee's job is to help them.

Getting your customers inside the door is not enough. The success of your business depends on the quality of customer service you extend. Give the best of yourself to those customers and your business. If you advertise or imply a certain service, see that it is carried out. Don't misrepresent yourself. Give your customers what you promise and they will come back, bringing their friends and relatives with them. That's the simplest and cheapest way to advertise. It is a proven fact. It costs five times more in advertising to get a new customer than it does to keep an old customer happy and coming back to you. Also, it is much easier and usually you can make more money on repeat or referred business.

Some businesses are preferred over others because the customers feel comfortable and welcome. Customers who do not feel welcome and secure will do business elsewhere. There is nothing more annoying than walking into a business, only to be ignored while the employees stand idly around talking to each other. If their annoyance is great enough, those customers will not patronize that business again. But when customers walk into a business where an employee greets them promptly with a smile, calls them by name, and gives them good service, the personal attention alone will help bring those customers back. Your customers are your business. They owe you nothing. If you or your employees give poor service, all the money you spend on advertising and promotion will be wasted. Everyone enjoys personalized attention, and it costs so little. If you are determined to give efficient service and attention, the field is wide open for your success. Keep your customers' interests number one in your mind. Treat your customers as people, not as commodities.

Once you have trained your help, listen to them. Employees often come up with good, useful ideas, and if they are given the chance to get involved, they will have more incentive to work well. Also, employees who realize your business is growing, and that promotions are available to those who do well, will work harder. When your employees do well, let them know it.

BOOKKEEPING

The next two questions you must answer are: How extensive a bookkeeping system do I need? What do I do if I don't know bookkeeping?

Your bookkeeping system is vital to your business. When followed correctly, it gives you a good working knowledge of how your business is doing throughout the year. If you are in retail sales, it can help you determine what inventory to order. No matter what type of business you have, you can see through your bookkeeping which areas are making you the most money, and where you can afford to cut expenses.

It is important to have a good, workable system which you control. If you don't know how to do books, you must learn. Keep them simple and understandable. If you want to set up your own books, there are various commercial forms available for purchase, and there are "how to" books which explain simplified bookkeeping systems. It might be wise to go to your local office supply and pick up some business forms to study and use. For instance:

> Spread sheets
> Profit and Loss Statements
> Financial statement
> Ledgers for general bookkeeping
> Inventory sheets

Be careful you do not get into trouble because you don't understand your bookkeeping system. Spend time with it daily, and go over your books carefully at least once a month. From the beginning, you must know what your expenses are and learn how to utilize your capital. Growing with your bookkeeping system will enable you to continue understanding it as your business becomes more involved. Using it correctly will help you keep a close, critical eye on the structure of your business.

In the beginning you should not need a full time bookkeeper, but as your business grows you may need to hire one. If your bookkeeper offers suggestions on how you can change your bookkeeping system to make it more efficient, be sure the changes, if any, are the way you want them. Remember, your books are for you to use and understand.

Eventually you may need to hire an accountant. A CPA can be a great help to you as you grow. They can provide you with a computerized printout each month, showing the percentages of your expenses and itemize all your financial activity. If you watch this information closely and spend enough time studying it, you will be able to lower some of your expenses without hurting your business, thus giving you a better net income. Your CPA can also provide you with a yearly financial statement, which will be required by your banks and creditors. Keep a copy on hand. Go over it carefully and know where you stand financially. Use it as the basis of your financial strategy.

GETTING AND USING ADVICE

There will always be new questions which need answers while you are organizing and operating your business, especially if you want it to be well-known and profitable. If, while forging ahead in your business, you run into a snag you don't expect, never be ashamed, afraid, or bashful to ask advice from more experienced or more successful people. Free advice can be more valuable than paid-for advice, and while you are gaining this knowledge, you are honoring the person you are asking.

You can often get good, honest, sound, free advice from your CPA, your banker, or a close business associate, but you still must be cautious, and you must use your own judgment. Don't automatically use the advice without thinking it through and planning its implementation. Relate it to your business situation, and use it as a tool. If it will not benefit you, discard it completely or file it away for use at a future time when it may apply.

12

WEARING DIFFERENT HATS

Let's assume you are now well on your way. Soon you will have enough extra capital to start investing in other areas, or expanding your business. We have reached the fun part of being successful. I like to call it venturing out, or "wearing different hats." It may not be mandatory that you wear different hats while going for the gold, but it is almost essential. A good example of what I call "wearing different hats" may best be described by sharing with you the many hats I wear in an average day, and for what purpose:

Hat #1 Getting up in the morning and doing my jogging and exercises. (Planning my day.)

Hat #2 Open up the office and be certain all the employees know what needs to be done. Take care of any problems that may have come up and make certain the business will run smoothly that day. Implement my dreams or priorities for the day.

Hat #3 Being a Director of a chain of banks, there are always special items to read and study, meetings to attend, and plans to be made.

Hat #4 Being a toy manufacturer, there are sales meetings, promotions, toy shows, and of course, the actual making of the toy to oversee.

Hat #5 The writing of this book has taken many hours of planning, studying, writing, and re-writing.

Hat #6 Owning mobile home parks presents problems which need to be taken care of, meetings with the managers, working out improvements, etc.

Hat #7 Selling mobile home parks through the real estate company involves contacting mobile home park owners, getting listings, and contacting prospects.

Hat #8 Almost daily, new investments and new real estate opportunities cross my desk. These need to be checked out and studied for two reasons. (1) to see if it would be a good investment for me, and (2) to keep myself current on what real estate is selling for and which locations are most active. This information may pertain to certain areas within my city, my city as a whole, the county, the state, nationally or internationally.

Hat #9 Studying the security market and the business world.

There are still other hats which I must wear at different times on different days. Hats for my investments in shopping strips, oil ventures, commercial properties and rentals, a mini-storage and office complex, and an almond orchard. Strange as it may seem, I do find time to relax and I do have a personal life that I am enjoying. I call this "wearing of many hats" my game of achievements. I like to see just how far out I can reach. My game of success was created years ago. This is what I am trying to inspire you to work towards as you start, plan, and watch your business grow.

You must create a game for yourself, a game of excitement which you are determined to win. Your overall game will be a combination of many moves, such as the move to create a better life for yourself, the move to enjoy what you are doing, the move to use your natural creativity, and the moves of accomplishments to win your game. Each move has its own unique hat, as well as its own adventure and problems. But it also offers its own type of self-fulfillment, commitment, and rewards. Like any other game, the rewards come from solving the problems.

Everything in life revolves around cycles. Business is no exception. Your business may be growing and you may be making good money. However, it is important that you be aware of and open to new possibilities. Prepare yourself when things are going well, so if necessary, you have something to fall back on. By doing this, you leave the door open for success in other fields. Then if your interest in your present business begins to decline or it becomes financially necessary to make a change, you have another field in mind. Do not depend on your business being good all the time. It won't be.

Determining how long you stay with your business is crucial to your financial success. Some people never lose interest in their business. Others have a time limit. A cycle of interest, if you will. Everyone's cycle is different. My cycle seemed to make a complete revolution every seven years. At the end of that time, I was usually ready for a change. So I either sold my business, expanded it, or changed it. Why? I needed the challenge to keep it interesting enough for me to put in those long, hard hours necessary to keep succeeding. Without the challenges and hard work, my business could have suffered, and I would not have been happy or successful.

When I sold my grocery store, I was making good money. But I needed to sell it because my interest in it had faded. I had been working hard a it for seven years, and I was getting bored. I needed new adventures. Boredom prevents efficient work effort. I knew if I stayed with it out of duty rather than out of pure interest, the business would go downhill.

How can you tell if it is time for a change? Do you have more interests outside your business than in it? Do you want to get away from it rather than to it? These are very good indicators. Are you bored? Do you find yourself dreaming about some other business which may take you higher in your financial planning? Has someone offered you a good price for your business? That may also be a signal that it is a good time to move on to a new venture.

Only you can determine when it is time for you to make that change. You have to determine your own cycle. But make certain you are going into something that will excite you and keep your interest, something you are good at and will make you the money you want. You cannot make a change just to make a change.

Eventually you may feel you have reached the limit. You have expanded as much as possible at your present location. You find yourself losing interest because the "fun" part of the game is not there anymore. Expanding to other locations may create enough interest and new ideas to keep you enthused.

The benefits of expansion are that you are staying in a field you know, and your employees are already trained. Employees who see promotions down the line will have the incentive to work harder. Because you have already trained them to do your work your way, their training will fit naturally into the new locations.

Be certain the people you train and then place in management at your new location are ready to meet the new responsibilities. Be sure they want to work the hours it will take to make the business a success. So often, expansion can hurt a business rather than help it, if the management is not strong.

Finally, do not squelch new ideas or new ventures. You never know. That new idea or possibility you are thinking about today could be the key to your financial success tomorrow.

If you feel your new interest will do better economically than your present business, do not be afraid to venture into it. Have confidence in yourself. A new hat is like medicine for when you start losing interest. When your business feels out of sorts, just reach for another hat. That hat will give you the incentive to perk up and make the game interesting enough to be fun again. It gives you the enthusiasm and interest you used to have.

As you strive to win the game, you will gain strength, get to know yourself better, and learn how to best utilize your abilities. This game of succeeding is a game of seeing how far you can stretch your mind, your thoughts, your creativity, and your imagination. In other words, how far can you stretch yourself? How many hours can you work? How successful can you be in how many different fields?

The accumulation of more wealth is not the only objective in succeeding. I try on many hats because each one interests and excites me and gives me a new outlook on life. This "wearing of many hats" is really a game of win or lose, and I want to see how many moves I can make that will help me win the game. Playing it keeps me alert and young. I feel like I am on top of the world. I know I won't win all the time, but even when I lose, I feel I have gained knowledge and excitement.

Everyone who has ever had the chance to be in this situation realizes they constantly have to make new decisions. As you move toward success, you will try on different hats, accept the challenges represented and make them work. And you, too, will find you will not be playing this game for the money alone but because you want to win. If the rewards come in the form of money, you will accept it just as anyone would, but your accom-plishments will actually be reward enough. Where else can you find or create so much excitement, have life so rewarding, and have so much fun?

The more attention you pay to your business when you start out, the earlier you get to play this game of "wearing hats". The people who are successful today have paid their dues. They played to win, and win they did! And because they played at the game and won, they accepted the rewards. If you want to play the game, you, too, must first pay your dues.

My interests have been mentioned to give you direction and inspiration. They are examples of what can be done by anyone. Each hat is, in its own way, just as exciting as the other. Strangely enough, no matter how many hats I'm wearing, I'm always trying on different hats. To me, this is what Reaching for the Gold is all about; playing the game, making as many moves as possible, wearing as many hats as possible, and winning as often as possible.

Why not fit yourself in different hats and create your own excitement by making winning moves?

13

GOING FOR THE GOLD

I would like to relate to you "My Onion Story." It happened when I was a young man, full of energy and ambition. I was very willing to work. Although I was a real estate broker, I wasn't making enough money to support my family and get ahead as fast as I wanted. I had just come out of the military service and was struggling hard to succeed, but because I did not have the money to rent a well-located office, I worked from a small office off the beaten path.

The young man working for me informed me his brother wanted to sell his farm equipment, which consisted of a garden tractor, a plow, and a disc. He also had about forty acres rented which he had used the previous year for growing onions, and from which he had made a small fortune.

He asked me if I wanted to buy the equipment and grow onions, and my answer was, "Yes! Anytime I can make money like that I would love to. But I don't have the money. How about if we go in partnership?"

So we decided that between the two of us we could scrape together enough money to buy the equipment and the seed. We knew we would have to do most of the work in the field ourselves.

We purchased the equipment and went out to start the plowing and seeding. I knew a little about farming, but absolutely nothing about the onion business. My partner knew a little about the onion business, but not much.

Everything was going fine, until one morning my partner came to me and said, "I'm sorry, but I'm going to have to leave. I'm in the Army Reserve, and they have called me up."

I said, "But, wait a minute! What about the onions?"

He replied, "Well, you're going to have to take over."

He offered to sell me his share. I explained to him I didn't have much money and didn't know how to go about finishing the onions. He told me I would learn, which wasn't very reassuring to me. I paid him a few hundred dollars for his share in the partnership and found myself out in the onion field.

Keep in mind that I continued selling real estate. Not only that, I had approached the local savings and loan with an idea to build a few houses under the FHA plan. The idea sounded good to them and they agreed to finance. I hired carpenters who were coming from Texas, and we started building five low-cost houses. (I feel I should stop and tell you now that up to this point I had never built anything).

Needless to say, I was busy. My day usually went like this: I got up around 4:30 a.m., had my breakfast, got in my little, old, beat-up, pick-up truck and took a drive down Front Street in Fargo, North Dakota, where the homeless hung out. In the morning, the ones who were hungry and in need of money would look for work. Local farmers hired them for the day. Each morning I would hire ten to fifteen men to hoe weeds. One man was chosen to be foreman. His job was to keep track of the other men and the number of rows they hoed.

Once I got them settled in the field, I buzzed back through town to the construction job, where my contractors were starting work on the houses. After making sure they were lined up for the day, doing their jobs, I went to my real estate office.

Sometime during the day, I would have to go to the bank and pick up money in dollar bills and change to pay my farm workers, who always got paid by the day. While taking time for this, I would check on my building project. The hours between all this activity were devoted to selling real estate.

Around 4:30 or 5:00 p.m., I would return to my onion field, get in the back of my truck, and the foreman of the day would give me a tally sheet on each man. We would figure out the men's wages, and I would pay them. They were paid according to the number of rows they hoed and usually only earned two to four dollars a day. After that, I would take them back into town.

After dropping the workers off, I would hurry home, have a bite to eat, rush out to my onion field, crank up my little tractor, and go up and down the field cultivating between the rows. Fortunately, my little tractor had lights on it, as I sometimes worked until one or two o'clock in the morning. I still remember cranking up my tractor and my singing voice. Away I would go, singing, "I'm a Lonely Little Petunia in an Onion Patch," riding up and down those rows, happy as could be. I was doing what I liked best: working hard and building my future.

The next day was exactly the same, over and over again, all summer. By the time fall came, my onion crop was huge. I went to town and bought some gunny sacks. I don't remember how many onions I had, but I had bags and bags of them. I was very lucky.

The price of onions that year was low, so I asked advice from some local onion growers. They suggested I hold on to my onions, saying I would get a better price for them in the spring. I explained to them I didn't have appropriate storage as they did. They told me all I had to do was find a barn, keep it warm so the onions wouldn't freeze, and by early spring I would come out a lot better.

So, taking their advice, I rented a barn that stood right next to my onion field. At least the location was good. I wouldn't have to transport them. I bought some old canvas and rope to construct some partitions. First, I divided off that old barn with the sway-back roof and walls that were buckled with age, into separate rooms with the rope. Then I threw those huge pieces of canvas over the ropes and hoped their weight wouldn't make the barn collapse. Finally, I stacked all those hundreds of sacks of onions in the barn. To keep it warm, I purchased some pot-bellied stoves and many cords of wood. A pot-bellied stove was placed in each divided room and I hired an old gentleman to keep the fires burning all winter.

Winter in North Dakota was severe that year, as usual. When spring finally came, instead of onion prices being higher, they were even lower than before. As luck would have it, Texas had harvested a bumper crop early that spring. So there I was, sitting with all those thousands of onions, waiting and waiting as the market grew weaker and weaker, not really knowing what to do as the weather turned warmer.

Then the miracle I had been waiting for happened. One bright, sunny day in June, two men walked into my office and said they heard I had some onions I wanted to sell. I said, with some emphasis, "You better believe it!"

So we drove out to the barn, but I was not prepared for what I was about to discover. My little old gentleman was gone. There had been a weather change during the last two weeks, and because it had gotten too warm in the barn, the onions had started to sprout. Each sack of onions had long, green sprouts sticking out. Needless to say, I lost my whole crop of onions.

If I had not gambled that the price of onions would be higher in the spring, I would have been much better off. By doing so, I created much more work for myself, a lot more expense, and I ended up with nothing.

Of course, that wasn't the end of it. I still had to dispose of all those smelly onions. Have you ever smelled a rotten onion? Little by little, using my old, beat-up, pick-up truck, I hauled my investment out to the county dump.

That was only part of my problem. During the winter months, no work could be done on the houses, but the contractor wanted an advance. So I made arrangements to pay him and his workers. When the weather permitted again, they finished the houses and departed for Texas. After they had gone, I discovered the outside shakes had been put on about two inches too far apart by FHA specifications. Because of that, the houses could not be sold with FHA-approved loans. The contractors could not be located, and because I had paid them in advance, I lost that money. To compound problems, I was left with only one recourse, to sell the homes by conventional loan. That was, indeed, difficult to do. Everything in those days was sold under the Federal Housing Administration. I just about broke even on the houses, after working nearly all year building them and getting them ready for sale.

By this time I was very far in debt. Now, in those days bankruptcy was out of the question. It took me a long time to pay those bills off, but I never gave up. I kept on planning and dreaming, working harder than ever to repair the damages, until finally I was out of debt again.

When I had paid my bills off after that disastrous year and had saved some money again, I bought a basement. I didn't have enough money to build a top on it, so I put some tar paper on the roof to prevent leakage, put on a sub-floor, and partitioned off some rooms down below. Once it was livable and rented, I put it up for sale. With the few hundred dollars profit from the sale, I purchased another little house, fixed that one up, rented it, and sold it. By utilizing patience, endurance and time, my capital gradually grew.

The buying, renovating and selling of homes enabled me to save enough for a small down payment, which in turn made it possible for me to purchase my grocery business. I had started to climb my mountain and had reached another very important plateau.

Although those two financial disasters seemed like the worst tragedies that could have ever happened to me, they were actually stepping stones to my success. No one could have convinced me of that while I was going through it, but that period in my life was one of my best educational experiences. I learned more about business in that one year than any university could have taught me in many years. As a result, I became a very good businessman. There is always a certain amount of luck involved in life. There are times when, no matter how hard you work and plan, at the end it just does not work out. But the more planning and working you do, the luckier you will be.

We are put on this earth to succeed and accomplish goals, but success is never easy. Don't expect to go through your life and have all your goals fall into place. It won't happen. Prepare yourself for hard knocks, and use them as your stepping stones to reach for the next plateau. If these stones are planted securely enough, you will reach your goal.

When you are discouraged, remember this story, and learn from your situation. Experiencing difficulties, if you are teachable and can learn from them without giving up, will make you a better person. They toughen you and make you cautious, making you understand that every deal is not sweet. To be a successful person, you must be prepared to move forward under any circumstances. I like to call it the school of hard knocks.

During this time of hardship, I realized planning is the key to a successful investment, not just going into something because it "sounds good." Throughout this chapter, I will share other personal experiences I have had in investments. While some of them paid off extremely well, others could have been disastrous if I had let them defeat my will to be successful.

How successful you become will depend on the amount of time you devote to it. As in daydreaming, you must develop a strategy for investing. An investment cannot be hit or miss. It must be studied, carefully thought out, and understood.

Planning also involves gaining enough knowledge to decide whether an investment is good before you invest. When you take time to study and plan your investment, you will feel more relaxed after you have made it. Do not make an investment you feel you will regret, or one that will cause you to lose sleep because of worry. Never let anyone push you into an investment which makes you feel uncomfortable. Plan ahead, be advised, and use your own judgment.

Your planning should begin now. Educate yourself. Study your investment opportunities. Attend classes or seminars which deal with securities, real estate, and business. Read newsletters to keep in touch with the world of investment. Study your local newspapers. Keeping up to date on real estate values and local economic progress will enable you to plan your investments effectively. Take advantage of local social activities, visit with friends and business acquaintances, listen to the news, and keep yourself informed. Then when the time is right for you and you have money to invest, you will be better prepared to determine if the investment is good or bad.

If, in your studying, you have gained an understanding of real estate, and you feel comfortable in that area, invest in commercial or income properties which will pay you rent each month. If you understand the stock market, then invest in securities which will pay you dividends. Any investment decision in your planning must be based on your likes and dislikes, as well as your knowledge of a particular investment. The more informed you are, the more success you will have making your investments.

Get your money working for you by investing it early, and learn as you grow. Train yourself to think of your money as an untiring employee that works for you day and night, costs you nothing, gives you no problems, and even works on weekends or during vacations. Once you have invested your money, it can pay you big dividends with little or no work effort on your part, and it is your key to becoming successful. But don't expect an immediate return.

Above all, be patient. If you don't know where to invest just now, put that extra cash into a savings account which can earn you interest, while cultivating a good business relationship with your bank. New investors sometimes feel that once they start to look, they have to make the decision to buy immediately. This is not true. You may have to look for years before you find a good buy. Business is a lot like a poker game. Each player is dealt a hand, but in order to win, you may have to wait a long time for a winning hand. The same principle holds true when you are making investment decisions. You cannot afford to take chances on poor investments.

Remember, we are not just planning your investments, we are also planning your future. Each person has different goals in life. Just because an investment is good for one person does not necessarily mean it is a good investment for you. Your investments must correspond with your lifetime goals and plans.

Listening closely to what investment brokers have to say regarding an investment and taking their advice is important in becoming a successful investor. But just because a broker is with an investment firm does not mean that person is qualified. Many times brokers do not know all the specifics of their commodity. Sometimes their suggestions are influenced by the amount of commission they will earn. Keep in mind, they are using your money and have nothing to lose. Whether you gain or lose, they are going to get paid. You can't make quick decisions, or depend completely on investment firms to make the right decisions for you.

All brokerage firms are not self-seeking. Some are reliable, but you should know about those which are not and avoid them. This warning applies to every investment you consider which involves a salesperson. Think twice. Be very careful. Don't depend on others, depend on yourself. It was you who got you this far. Don't be afraid to listen and take advice, but be informed enough to weed out the nonprofitable investments and make your own responsible decisions. You be the boss.

The same is true when buying real estate. The more real estate you study, the more prepared you will be when a good investment comes along. But you still have to be careful. A salesperson's job is to sell you whatever they are selling. Some do not present all the facts. At other times, they may not even know all the facts. It is your responsibility to search for those facts yourself.

Sometimes an investment will be sold to you on the basis of tax advantage.

I have a friend, a CPA, who always says, "Give me the income. I'll pay my taxes."

I have another friend who says, "Give me an investment that gives me a fifty percent tax break, and I will gamble that the investment will pay off at least as much."

One particular oil venture was sold to me on the basis of tax advantages plus profit, by a top man in one of the leading investment firms. Grant you, neither he nor the firm knew oil prices were going to drop. But, when I look back, I wonder why I didn't invest that money where I could control it. Although getting a tax break is worth consideration, sometimes it is better to pay the taxes and invest in a field which is familiar to you, one you understand.

I would have been much better off through the years to have taken the first friend's advice, and invested my money in ventures I could control and were related to my natural ability. Of course, that would have taken more time and work. Strangely enough, people always seem to be lazy, and try to find the easy way to make a dollar. Your author is even guilty of that.

Never let a broker or salesperson push you into making a premature decision. If a costly investment is being considered, it will take more than a couple days to work out the details. Don't decide too quickly. If you do, your chances of making the wrong decision are more likely. You have to look and listen, then investigate the situation. Be sure the investment is right for you. In other words, do your homework.

Looking for investments is exciting. I study them while listening closely to people, but I make my own decisions. If they start to pressure me, I tell them to give me the facts, not a sales pitch, and then give me time to sit down and figure out whether the investment is good for me. I want to hear what they have to say. If the offer is good, I will know it. It is amazing what a few days thinking, figuring, and considering can do to help you make up your mind about that possible investment. If they tell me it will be sold in a few days, I tell them to keep me in mind for something else.

Salespeople have a pet statement, "If you don't buy it today, it will be gone tomorrow." Don't let this kind of statement influence your decision to buy. Be prepared for it.

An investor with little experience is often the target of fast-talking brokers or sales representatives. They always make the deals look super, and the salespeople, being professionals, assure you they are super. But let me warn you now, making-big-money-fast schemes just do not work. Be careful! No matter how closely you check it out, the result is usually unprofitable.

I have found through the years, when someone earning a commission is trying to sell me something, they are always my friend. This "friend" can be very convincing. I cannot depend on them to check it out for me, because they have not given me the information as friendly advice. Whenever there is a commission involved, or the other party is getting paid, it is solely your responsibility to take your time and check it out, friend or no friend.

Consider this example. Suppose a friend comes to you and tells you he has found a good investment. Would you like to go in with him on it? If he is sharing this with you strictly because he is your friend who wants to share his good find with you, or needs a partner in this investment, that is good. However, you still need to check out the opportunity. If he tells you he is, in any way, receiving compensation, whether by reduction of price or being paid a commission or finder's fee, then you, for your own protection, must check the investment out more thoroughly.

If you feel extremely uncomfortable or vulnerable when speaking with brokers and salespersons, there is an alternative for investment counseling which you may not have considered. Your banker. Your banker has been trained in investments and can give you unbiased assistance, because he is not receiving a commission for helping you.

Maintain your own ideas and think things out for yourself, but never be afraid to listen to helpful hints and suggestions which will help in your planning, not only for the present, but also for the future.

Obviously, the aim of this book is to give you guidance in becoming successful and making money. Sound money comes from working hard, investing constantly, and saving consistently. Making money slowly is always the best and surest way. If you invest a large amount of money in one investment, and it is not successful, the results could be disastrous for you. It is a simple fact. The fewer mistakes you make in investing, the more successful you will become.

I want to share an example with you about a friend of mine who sold his very successful business a few years ago and invested his money in a venture with someone he didn't know. The venture was located in another state, and he lacked a general knowledge of the business, but he was sure the investment was going to be profitable. His partner assured him of high returns for high investment, and greediness prompted him to risk all.

He had become so successful, he felt he was invincible and that failure could not touch him. Within two years he had lost around ten million dollars, plus an annual income of nearly a million dollars. Today he is broke. When you have achieved success, it is easy to become greedy and not do your homework, thus ending up in this type of situation.

Being wealthy and successful is no excuse for investing un-wisely in fields you know nothing about. Some people prefer to invest in areas unfamiliar to them. For instance, let's assume that someone is doing very well in their chosen business. Instead of using that knowledge wisely and investing in the same type of business, they choose to take their hard-earned money and invest it in ventures which they cannot control and in partnerships with people they do not know. As a result, their chances of losing becomes much greater.

If you have been unwise enough to do that in the beginning, I hope you lost a few deals. Not to put you down forever, but to make you stop and think. Those losses should have made you a better investor. That is practical, useful education. Using that practical education should enable you to make better investments.

In Chapter Twelve, we talked about cycles. There are also cycles in the field of investments, which means their value is increasing or decreasing. Some are predictable, most are not. Many people invest when an investment is paying top dollar, only to get caught on the way down and lose.

These cycles can be referred to as trends. By studying the trend, or general direction of an investment, you can determine whether that particular investment should be profitable. An investment of any sort should never be made without close scrutiny of the trends or signals which occur in your daily business world. Take time to look for them and study them. It will save you money and headaches.

Trends in real estate are determined by the interest rates and building tendencies. If the area you are interested in has attracted many new businesses, it is a good area in which to invest. Real estate is most profitable in cities which are growing, or the surrounding suburban areas of established cities. The need for housing or industrial/business developments, coupled with the current interest rates, are determining factors. When industry moves into your area, and the need for housing or other businesses increases, land prices usually rise. If you find a need for the type of real estate you are interested in, or better yet, when there is a need for a certain type of real estate and low interest rates are available, that should be a determining factor to go ahead with your real estate plan. Of course, you must watch that the area is not being over-built.

When looking for trends in securities, the same principal applies, only in reverse order. If you know of a company whose stock is down, and you know why it's down, it may be a good investment for you.

For instance, a local bank may have been in difficulty because of too many real estate failures. You know the problem has been corrected, because the real estate has been sold, and the loan officers who had caused the problem are no longer with the firm. You know the new loan officers are good, reputable people, and you also know the new management is knowledgeable in banking. In this type of situation, you should invest, while the stock is deflated. With all those positive signals, the stock's value can only rise.

REAL ESTATE

Real estate transactions are the largest money arrangements most people will ever make, from buying a home or a business to purchasing commercial and income properties. Learn as much as you can about the real estate business, and understand the values of property. Whether you ever get your license or not is unimportant, but it is good to have the knowledge, there are so many directions to pursue, and a wise investment will be to your advantage, no matter what business you are in.

You could make more from your investments than you can by working. The more you know, the better informed you will be when making them. There are very few people who take time to learn about them and understand them. I want you to know as much as possible, so you can judge opportunities for yourself. The less you have to depend on others, the better off you will be. I prefer investing in real estate, because I feel the best opportunities are there. But not understanding them could, in the end, cost money rather than make money.

I have known doctors, attorneys, and prominent business people who are very successful in their fields who have worked most of their lives paying off unprofitable investments. This is mainly because they did not understand enough about the investments they made. Had they been better prepared to make qualified decisions, and not relied on someone who was working for a commission, they most likely would not have invested unwisely. So, prepare yourself, and learn to rely on yourself. This is where "educating yourself forever" comes in.

You have dreamed your dreams, set your goals and plans, and have even taken time to get advice on what types of investments are available. You have accumulated some money and are now ready to invest. What do you do? You will have financial advisors calling you, stockbrokers camped on your doorstep, and stacks of mail delivered to your office each day. Everyone has a tip for you and wants to spend your money. Most of them will tell you how to make a fortune fast. I always ask myself, "If they know so much, why aren't they rich?"

Your investment goal is to build your estate for the future. Where you decide to invest your money is totally up to you, but you should be looking for capital gains and income. Real estate with income is an excellent choice, because it helps pay for itself. It will increase in value if you have bought correctly, and is a good hedge against inflation.

Be patient. It may take a long time to find the "right property" for sale. But whatever you do, don't give up. Keep looking. When you finally find it, set up your plan and make your offer, and then determine to spend time making your plan and offer work. It may take weeks, or even months, plus a lot of effort, to purchase that property at your terms.

A good real estate investment can be worth a fortune to you. It is worth spending time working to purchase it for the right price and terms. If you are buying the property through a real estate firm, do not let a broker talk you into buying the property as it is listed. Even if it is a good buy, you may be able to purchase it at a better price, or with better terms. I prefer working with the seller personally, but there are times when you may have to have a real estate broker involved. If you have a good knowledgeable broker who will work hard for you, it can be advantageous. There again, you must still be in charge; you must be the boss.

If you lose a deal because the seller won't accept your offer, don't get discouraged. Keep on looking. I cannot stress enough the importance of being patient when buying real estate. With patience and determination, you will eventually find the "right property," at the right terms, making it all worthwhile.

A really good opportunity in real estate or securities may only come around once or twice in a lifetime. It may happen tomorrow, or next year, or maybe not for many years. I want you to realize this and have enough patience to wait. Continue to look, study, plan, and prepare. Then when the opportunity presents itself, you will recognize it and have the money to invest, as well as the confidence and knowledge needed to identify it as a good investment. Patience is the name of the game. When the chance does come, it makes the waiting all worthwhile.

Real estate investments, initially, can be made on your own with your own capital, and for your own gain. Borrowing for real estate ventures is usually safe, because you can sit down and figure out what your actual income and expenses will be. To initiate your investments, you could begin by buying a small, inexpensive house, fixing it up, and selling it. Or you could, if you are young enough, buy a piece of corner property at a busy intersection, or where an intersection will be someday, and then sit back and wait. When that property increases in value because of location, you might make more money off that one investment than you could make by working. Choosing the right location, getting the right financing, and buying it at the right price is the key.

Remember that piece of property across the street from my little trailer park, which I envisioned as the perfect spot for my expanded sales lot, as well as an investment for the future? Because I could not afford the down payment and the monthly payments all at one time, I purchased that land in four stages. After using the property for approximately fifteen years as a sales lot, obtaining my income from it, and using the interest on the loan as a write-off, I leased the land for a shopping strip for fifty years. Now I receive a very pleasant monthly income, with a rent increase due me every five years. This example in itself should explain why it is important to study and save for the right investment.

By committing myself to making payments on that property for years, I accomplished three things: I saved the principal each month; I deducted the interest from my taxes; and I didn't have my money sitting idle, making it easier for me to spend on personal luxuries.

The example above demonstrates how valuable a wise real estate investment can be. Once you have trained yourself to find and recognize when an investment is good for you, then you are ready to invest. You must train yourself to know when to buy and how to make the most profit from that property. You must also know when to sell, lease, or make changes.

If making money through real estate investments is your aim, the key factor will be your ability to make an offer on the property which is advantageous to you, rather than just paying the asking price. Keep in mind, the asking price is usually higher than the seller actually hopes to get. You should never purchase a piece of real estate without making an offer. (In fact, you should never purchase any major item without making an offer.)

Never hesitate to make an offer. Some people are afraid of hurting the seller's feelings, or being turned down. These are illogical excuses. Making an offer costs you nothing.

Knowing how much someone is motivated to sell will help you tremendously in making your offers. Many people are desperate to sell. They may have to sell because it is taking up too much of their time. Maybe they have another deal going and need the money. Other reasons which motivate people for coming down in price and give you a hint for a good buy could be divorce, estate settlement, or job transfer. These are just a few examples.

Make your offers low enough. If, when you make your offer, the seller doesn't agree, never let yourself feel you need what they are selling. Train yourself to sit back and relax. If they are not interested in that offer, they will let you know and probably make a counter offer. If they do, this does not mean you have to agree to it. Never pay more than you really feel the property is worth. Just because a seller makes a counter offer does not necessarily mean they will not accept your original offer.

Your best advantage is to stay where you are for a while and play the game of "bluff", just as you do in that poker game we talked about earlier. If they do not move, leave your name and phone number with them, so they can contact you if they change their minds concerning your offer. By doing that, you let them know you are still interested but want the property on your terms. If they don't call you, go back in a couple days, and make your offer again. If they still won't take it, you may have to reconstruct your offer, but don't do so unless all the terms are favorable. Tieing up your money in an unfavorable deal means you will not have the money to invest if a better investment does come along.

If you don't finalize a deal, don't worry about it. It simply means you weren't supposed to have it. Keep looking and watching until the right investment comes along. Remember, there are numerous investments out there. When you buy property for the right price and the terms are good, you won't have to worry when and if you decide to sell. The value will be there. But if you purchase property at too high a price, and the terms are not favorable, it could become a problem instead of a good investment.

Making offers is another name for buying with conditions. When making any large real estate purchase, it is usually wise to buy with conditions. In other words, make your offer subject to terms. There are many incentives you can use to influence your seller. For instance, offer a balloon payment due in x number of years; or buy with a lease-option plan; or offer to purchase the property with a variable or increasing payment plan. If you have done your homework, the price is satisfactory, and your down payment and conditions are acceptable, then you have a good deal.

Sometimes you may have to change a condition to get what you want. For instance, suppose the seller wants $100,000 for his property with $20,000 down, and he will carry the balance at ten percent for thirty years. But you would like to purchase the property for $75,000, and you only have $10,000 to pay down. If your income is sufficient, and your credit is good, you could make the seller this offer: $75,000 purchase price, $10,000 down payment, another $10,000 balloon payment in five years, and payment in full within ten years. At that time, you may have enough cash to pay it off, or you may want to go to a bank and refinance the property. Because the seller is getting paid off in full sooner, they may be influenced to accept your offer.

Learning to make offers that work only comes through practice. Practice making bids on everything, until you become an expert and making offers comes naturally. Practice will make your offers tactful and inoffensive, as well as convincing. The seller will think that your offer is actually the value of their property or merchandise. You can save a tremendous amount of money in a lifetime just by making offers. The money you save can be used for other investments.

SECURITIES

As for investments in securities, find yourself a good, hard-working broker, who shares your ideas concerning investing. Keep yourself well-informed. Study the market and watch for trends in the economy. Look for companies which have solid management and a good track record. Study individual stocks for yourself. Watch them closely for trends and signals and be aware of their rating. When you have prepared yourself and feel you are ready to invest, be sure you have good, solid, more-than-hearsay facts you have gathered on your own. Train yourself to be overly cautious. There is money to be made, but there is also money to be lost.

Stock and bond investments are generally associated together. If you are in a high tax bracket, one profitable way to invest is in tax-free bonds. When buying, invest money you feel you will not need for some time. Bonds should be considered a long-range investment. Tax-free bonds pay you a percentage on the interest earned either monthly, quarterly, or yearly. I prefer the bond funds which pay monthly. Imagine getting a tax-free paycheck every month! Super! Sometimes I wish all my money was invested in that manner. (Keep in mind, I am not writing this book to give advice on what investments you should make.)

Educate yourself concerning bond investment. Listen, but don't depend solely on your stockbroker. Be sure your bonds are well protected and their rating is good.

In any stock or bond investment, avoid option situations where the brokerage carries the balance to a later date, at which time you have to pay it off. Borrowing money to buy securities is a poor policy.

Very seldom have I been able to find a security which paid enough dividends to support paying interest on that money. What if the value of the security declines? You still owe the debt. If you don't have the money to invest in the beginning, what makes you think you are going to have enough money to repay that debt, if your investment drops in value? No matter how convincing your broker sounds, there is no guarantee that a stock is going to rise in value. You are the only one who can protect yourself. My experience has proven an individual has more chances of making money in real estate than they do in the stock market.

No one is lucky enough to make every investment pay off. Sometime during your life, you will probably make a poor decision. It isn't quite as frightening when you have made your fortune, but if you are just starting out, making profitable investments can be a determining factor in achieving your success.

PARTNERSHIPS

Partnerships can cause you many problems and possibly great losses, if you are not extremely careful. Be sure you understand all your obligations and the laws of your state in regards to partnerships, before entering into a partnership agreement. A partnership is just that. Your control is limited, because you are not the sole owner/operator of your investment. Obviously, some are profitable, but caution is the key word.

Following are a couple examples of what can happen if you are not cautious when investing in partnerships.

A few years back, an acquaintance came to see me, and he told me about a customer who was coming into his bank with large deposits. Upon inquiry about the source of his money, the man replied it was from an oil venture in Kansas. My friend had checked into it, and said it looked like a good investment. He was considering investing and asked me if I was interested. I said I would be willing to check it out. We flew to Kansas, checked it out, thought it looked good and decided to invest.

At that time, the oil industry was booming, the tax credits were good, and all circumstances were perfect for investing. But we didn't know the man selling this partnership investment to us was dishonest. He didn't know any more about the oil business than I did. He went broke, then bankrupt, and as a result, I lost most of the money I had invested. To make matters worse, I found out later that this friend who gave me all this "valuable information" was receiving compensation for getting some of our other mutual friends and myself to invest in this partnership. If I had known this from the start, I might not have gone into the venture. I certainly would have checked it out more thoroughly.

A couple of years later, another investment firm offered an oil venture, and I invested over $100,000 in it. Just when everything was going as planned, oil prices dropped, making it a very poor investment. Had I taken this money and built another mobile home park, or invested in a project I had complete control over, I am certain I would have had much more profitable returns.

Choosing to go into a limited partnership in a business I did not know, or have any control over, caused me to lose valuable time and money. Through these ventures I learned to be wary of limited and general partnerships. General partnerships are the most dangerous, as you are responsible for all the liabilities which are put on the partnership. In comparison, if you are involved in a limited partnership, you will only be liable for the amount you invest. The greatest disadvantage of a limited partnership is that you have very little or no control over decisions made by the general partners.

At times, a partnership does have advantages. You can make sizable investments, or invest in larger properties, while investing less cash. If you are interested in a certain investment, but don't have enough capital to venture into it alone, you can make the investment with other people. You share the use of their capital and their knowledge, while getting a positive return on your partial investment. In making an investment with partners, each of you invests a certain amount of capital for a percentage of the investment, and each receives income based on that percentage of ownership.

Unfortunately, nearly all successful business persons insist on going into partnerships when they have already proven they are capable of earning and controlling their own money. My advice to you is to avoid partnerships whenever possible.

IN CONCLUSION

Making investments has, for me, been the fun part in this game of becoming successful. I contribute much of my success to the faith I have in myself and my ability to earn money. You have that ability as well. Just keep yourself so broke that you have to work to pay your payments on your investments. By doing that, your income starts working for you, because you have no time to spend it on unnecessary things. Staying in that cycle will eventually get you the lifestyle you want.

I still enjoy myself most when I am busy. Naturally, I enjoy trips and golfing, but even that can become boring after a while. But business? Never!! There are too many obstacles, too many variations, too many other business people to out-think, out-wit, out-smart, out-perform, out-work. There just isn't any time to become bored with that many variations and challenges confronting you.

Through the years, I have trained myself to make money and to make investments. Most people earn money but spend it too soon on personal items. Only when you have adequate money coming in do you want to splurge. How much will be taken out of the investment fund for personal items, and when, is an individual choice.

Whether you are just starting out, or have been in business for years, the dollars you make are very valuable. It will take you strenuous work and considerable time to accumulate those funds. The more you spend unnecessarily, the longer it will take you to fulfill your goals. If you spend too much, you will run out of time to accumulate it.

Let me stress again, you only have so much time to make money during your lifetime. It is essential to efficiently control both of these. Your key to success in business is to make sound financial decisions. Your business must come first. Learn how to invest your finances, just as you learn how to run your business and manage your time.

Here is my simple <u>Formula for Success.</u> I want you to read it, think about it, memorize it, and use it.

$$\text{HARD WORK} = \text{BUSINESS}$$
$$\text{BUSINESS} = \text{PROFITS}$$
$$\text{PROFITS} = \text{INVESTMENTS}$$
$$\text{INVESTMENTS} = \text{EXCESS INCOME}$$
$$\text{EXCESS INCOME} = \text{RICHES AND SUCCESS}$$

Apply this simple formula as you journey from plateau to plateau. Your investments will become adventures and your reward will be the self-satisfaction of succeeding.

14

COMMUNITY INVOLVEMENT

Having the time and money to join service clubs and local organizations, as a result of achieving success, is another fun part in your game.

The best way to get involved is by actually joining clubs or organizations. Many of these help your community work towards getting more businesses and making sure community activities are organized. My word of caution is, don't get so involved that you have no time for your own business. When first starting out, you will have very little time for organizations. Later, when the business is success-ful and does not require your being there all the time, you may want to join. If you say "yes" to too many organizations, you will use hours of valuable time, going to meetings and serving on committees, which you should be using to work your own business.

Every community has a variety of organizations. It might be wise to visit them before you decide to join. Taking part locally is a great way to promote your business, while helping these groups. You are provided with excellent opportunities to discuss problems, new ideas, and innovations with other prominent business associates. Being involved in your community allows you to meet new friends, broaden yourself socially, and have an enjoyable diversion from daily routine.

It is important to know what is going on within your community and in your local area. There is no better way to find these things out than to associate with the business community. If you join the right organizations, you will not only be helping out, but you will be benefiting your business. You may join because your friends are in the group, but your main purpose should be to meet new people and become involved in community affairs.

Another way to get involved in your community is by making donations. There are many organizations which depend on financial assistance to promote their programs. If you make your donations wisely, you will help the needy and also bring benefit to your own business.

When should you, the new business entrepreneur, take time to get involved, and how much time should you allot to this type of activity? Your decision depends on your personality and type of business. It is unfair to live in a community, earn your living from it, and not put anything back into it.

Maybe you have thought about becoming involved in politics on the local level. This decision is a totally private matter. Although it is community involvement, it will probably detract from your business rather than enhance it. If you have positive ideas which will be helpful to the progress of your community, and these ideas cannot be heard without your becoming politically involved, then you may have to enter the political arena.

Before you do, consider this. Politics can and will demand much of your time. You may find, at the end of your campaign or stint in office, your business, which took so much time to build, may have actually suffered or failed, rather than benefited. You will have to weigh your decision carefully. If the decision is in favor of running for political office, then provisions must be made to keep the business in tact and solvent.

In other words, you must learn to help yourself before you can help others.

15

LATER ON IN LIFE:
an Epilogue

You quit your job. You started your business. You worked very hard. You became successful. You invested and the investments were paying off. You took that money and invested some more. Now you are starting to get gray. You have money in the bank, a nice home, a new car. Everything is going great. You have made it. You take your vacations, and when you return, your money is still coming in. You have done everything right. You have tried on different hats, accepted the challenges, and made them work. You paid your dues. People tell you your success has been earned and offer their congratulations. What can be wrong with that? You say, "I am a success. Everything is going great." You have power. You can do anything, buy anything. People respect you. (At least, you think they do.) You are happy. You have paid your dues.

Do you remember that in the beginning of the book I told you to find a snowbank, step into it, then step backwards, and look at your footprints? Then I wanted you to ask yourself a question: "How well do I know that person?" Now that you are a success, I want you to find that snowbank, step into it again, then step back, and look afresh at those footprints. What kind of person are you today? Do you like what you are? Do you feel good about yourself? How many people did you hurt, on your way to the top? Have you changed? Have you made any promises that you didn't keep? Did you lose any friends over it? How do your children feel? How does your spouse feel? Are they still proud of you? Do they still love you? More importantly, do you still love yourself?

You have money and success. What else do you have? Did you use your friends? Did you use your customers? Did you use your spouse or children? These are important questions. If you can answer them correctly, you are a very lucky, very smart person. If you can't answer them correctly, it may not be too late to make some changes.

One thing that is most important, while going through life on our way to riches, is that we do not lose sight of God. Without His friendship, we live for nothing, and we end up with nothing. I realize some of you who read this book do not believe in God, and although I admit you have the freedom of choice, I feel you are making a mistake by leaving God out of your life and your business. He has been a tremendous help to me.

As a young man, I was fortunate enough to be brought up in a family that believed in God, and I, like many other children, went to Sunday School and church regularly, as though it were a habit. Not until later in life did I realize its value.

I had four children, my real estate business was doing badly, my bills were piling up, my house payment was past due, and I really did not know where to turn. I had just listed an old two-story house that looked as though it was ready to collapse. The present owners used a step-ladder to get up to the opening of the second story.

I had made an appointment to show this so-called 'house' and was on my way to meet the prospective buyers. As I told you before, I was desperate. For some reason, I pulled over to the side of the road, got on my knees on the passenger side, and prayed that these people would buy this house.

To my surprise, and for no apparent reason, they did buy that house. Ever since that sale, God has been my Partner, a very good Partner.

I want to emphasize that success is your goal, but not success at any cost. You must conduct your business fairly, so you can look back over your life, be proud of your accomplishments, and be content with how you have gained your wealth. If, at the end of your lifetime, you cannot look back with pleasure at your success, then your success has been gained without merit.

This chapter, with its introspective questions and thoughts, may seem like a negative way to conclude. Actually, the opposite is true. I want you to use this chapter as a basis for conducting your business from start to finish. Most of you are going to be reading this book before you are successful. I want you to keep this chapter in mind as you journey through your world of success.

110

The profit you make from wise investments is one reward of hard work and constructive planning. Being rewarded by the knowledge that you have accomplished something may be more of a reward than becoming financially successful in itself. Do not spend all your life "doing" and, at the end of your life, feel like you have done nothing. Keep in mind there is more than one type of gold to attain.

Your gold can come in many different forms. It does not have to be money. It can come in the form of love, or joy, or mental well-being. It can come from doing what you enjoy, whether you are working or playing. Some people enjoy playing golf, but aren't good enough at it to make money. That does not stop them from enjoying the game. Maybe you enjoy painting, writing, or reading. If so, you should make time to do these things. By doing what you enjoy most, you are investing in yourself.

I want you to be successful, to have fun in succeeding, and to be completely satisfied with the results of your success. I want you to be able to smile and to be pleased with the person you have become. I want you to be proud of the person whose footprints you see. I want you to be content with the results of playing and succeeding in this game of success.

Someday you will wake up, look into the mirror, and find yourself to be an old person, wondering if you have accomplished enough, or if you have fulfilled most of your dreams. You will never accomplish everything you want, and you will never fulfill all your dreams, but if you can honestly say you are satisfied; you did try; you have not wasted your life, but lived it to the utmost; you helped others; you were not a burden on others; and, you were fair, then you have reached your goal for riches. You have, in reality, achieved your gold.

I want you to be able to say to yourself, "I reached for the gold, not the bronze, and I have attained it!"

THE END

111